MUGSHOTS

MY FAVORITE DETECTIVE STORIES

JOHN A. HODA

ALL THINGS INVESTIGATIVE

AUTOBIOGRAPHICAL, YES. MEMOIR, NO. I STILL HAVE MORE STORIES TO TELL

Mug Shots: My Favorite Detective Stories
By John A. Hoda

INTRODUCTION

"You oughta write a book about that."

I heard this regularly from friends and family for close to forty-two years. I arrived home from working cases and regale my family with my latest whodunit. I always had a good story to tell. Long after the dessert plates were cleared away, they would beg me for another one while I refilled my coffee mug from my collection of mugs gathered from around the world purchased in towns where my cases had taken me.

After graduating from college with a degree in Criminology, I quickly joined my local police department, before beginning my first career as an insurance fraud investigator.

When the opportunity presented itself, I obtained private investigator licenses in New York and Southern New England.

Along the way, I detoured into the highly-competitive roller-coaster ride of Forensic Genealogy (finding people who had no clue that they were entitled to large sums of money) and finally settled into working cases for attorneys who represented either the severely injured or for attorneys who stood up for the wrongfully charged or convicted.

I jump around through the decades.

I had to omit names and sometimes places to protect the innocent and not so innocent. Where my memory failed me on the minor points, I exercised dramatic license.

Is this an Autobiography? Hell no. Memoir? Nope. I still have some big cases brewing and still have a lot of gas in the tank. I just like telling stories and these are some of my favorites.

Enjoy!

'CUSE

'CUSE

I hate the smell of jet fuel in the morning. The other barely-awake business travelers and I received a stiff brace of eau de aviation octane when we walked out onto the Westchester County Airport tarmac. No jetway for us. The USAir puddle jumper had just arrived from The Big Apple to whisk us to Albany, Utica, Syracuse - my destination, then Rochester and finally Buffalo. Bouncing up and down in a crammed turbo-prop was not fun, but it sure beat thirteen hours of windshield time.

Was I complaining? Not really. This was my work and I loved it. I was hired as the first Special Investigator for an insurance company. I had the plum job of sniffing out bogus property or casualty claims. With claims offices throughout the East Coast and the Mid-West, I was hopping.

As we lurched into the sky that morning, I began to think about the case that dragged me out of a warm bed in my quiet suburban Connecticut home before dawn.

The insured owned an excavations company. He kept his

premiums down during the wintertime by taking some heavy equipment off his business policy. They would not be insured while they sat around inside his shop collecting dust waiting for the spring thaw. This year, when mud season ended, he added them back onto his policy, and a week later, his newest Bulldozer drowned in an irrigation pond. Luckily, just before it disappeared below the surface, the owner leaped to safety with all his limbs and his lunchbox intact.

Sure, the Insurance company would have gotten some salvage out of it, but $75,000 was still a big nut to pay, especially when the claim came in at the same time as the policy endorsement putting the dozer back on the policy. That was the red flag and it begged the question of which came first, the loss or the coverage. Did Mr. Insured have the good fortune of insuring the dozer before watching it slide slowly down an embankment into a pond or not? Did the agent do a favor for his client and back-date the policy coverage? Did the agent mess up by forgetting to make the endorsement and was now trying to cover his own ass?

Only one scenario was legitimate and the others were, quite simply, stealing; Felony Theft by Deception and Federal Mail Fraud- the kind of insurance fraud that I was an expert at uncovering. The steady throbbing of the engines allowed me to contemplate each combination in my mind. In order for the claim to be true, certain representations by the agent and the insured had to be verified. When my investigation was done, I would have a fairly good idea what really happened. I would constantly test the facts I unearthed against what they were saying. Good detective work, it's been said, is about using your imagination as much, if not more, than your shoe leather.

Insurance companies were slowly waking up to the fact

that Special Investigations could impact the bottom line, but it meant ex-cops like me working on the Claims floor. I came in talking the talk, then one case at a time, walking the walk. To tell the truth, it was more like a swagger. I had both the police training and the claims background. I combined six really fun years of investigating insurance fraud with three years as a field claims manager before taking on this challenge. I was slowly turning even the crustier claims adjustors into believers, but in this case, there was the added twist.

Was an agent playing fast and loose with the company's money? It did happen, but saying it out loud was almost unheard of. It didn't help that this agent was a regular at the million-dollar roundtable for his earned premiums. The marketing people and the underwriters were none too pleased that Claims would dare question the integrity of one of their prized agents. Turf wars like this were not uncommon when somebody's yearly bonus was riding on the outcome.

So, as my ears were popping with the descent into Syracuse Hancock International, I knew that very soon my rental car, a new 1990 Dodge Spirit compact, would take me to the cordial yet very-guarded producer of this policy where I would most likely get an another earful. We had already pushed a few pawns around the board when I set up the appointment to review his file and take his statement. It promised to be an interesting meeting.

On my way to the rental counter, I spied the gift store and made a quick detour. I'd hit it on the return trip as it had the requisite t-shirt for my son, a doll for my infant daughter, a local cuisine cookbook for my wife, who is a gourmet cook, and lastly, a Syracuse coffee mug for me.

I really liked coffee. I craved caffeine so much that if I

could hang an intravenous drip from the ceiling of my company car, I would have. I revved my engines on the stuff. I routinely drank out of mugs brought home from my travels; particularly from cities where I had hit the big home run. Each one reminded me of a good story. That helped on those mornings when I needed a little inspiration to go with my java jolt.

~

The South Salina Street Downtown Historic District in Syracuse or 'Cuse to the locals held a fading grandeur of years gone by. The agent's office furnishings reflected the sad feel of what once was. He made me sit the obligatory extra fifteen minutes in his outer office, which I completely understood as part of the head games we were playing. I would take exactly the same additional amount of time during his recorded statement while he fumed on the hot seat. Cooling my jets, I studied the awards, the pictures of him posing with other town mucked-y-mucks and the charity golf tournament foursomes. They were all dated from the Seventies and spoke of the importance of a once-upon-a-time downtown mover and shaker.

"How was your flight? Can I get you a cup of coffee? Please have a seat," he said, as he ushered me into his office. The rush of words and gestures hit me immediately as a prelude to the real or faked irritation of the busy businessman that he would try to portray later.

But I wasn't a rookie and I wasn't buying into it. Instead, I remained standing and marveled at his collection of fire-marks. In olden days, a fire-mark was the small sign that policyholders would place on their homes or businesses for the firemen to see. I spotted a real collector's item from the first American property insurance company, The Phil-adelphia Contributionship founded by Benjamin Franklin. I remembered that from my earliest training in the business. Agents collected fire-marks from companies for whom they wrote policies. It was a hobby and it showed how many different insurers trusted this agent. I purposely took my time gazing at them.

"Nice collection of fire-marks, some of them are real antiques," I said.

I took my time settling into the well-worn leather chair across from his walnut-engraved desk and then I finally made eye contact. He was older, but not ancient; wearing his pure silver hair a little long to let the world know that he still had plenty of it. Years of boozing and overeating showed in the busted veins on his nose and on his cheeks.

"The flight was painless, that's all you can ask for these days. I take it with cream and sugar, thanks," I said.

His suit was tired, but clean, as was his shirt and too-wide tie. He still had his pride and I would respect it throughout the interview. I'd be polite, but direct, without being blunt.

So the dance started and I led him through the recorded statement process. It was as much about learning about his insured and how the policy was generated as it was about capturing the agent's statements. We focused on his office processes and how it boiled down to his clerks noting the phone calls endorsing the heavy equipment and then a week later receiving the notice of loss. There was no other normal course of business records to corroborate this most important fact. No phone logs or sequentially numbered forms to mark the dates. He or they could have easily changed the notations in the file to reflect the given chronology of events in order to afford coverage. No checks were received in the mail, no envelopes with postmarks. He became more frustrated when his files could not produce the evidence that he was telling the truth.

I ended the statement noting the time and date and turned off the pocket recorder. I flipped it open and removed the mini-cassette tape, to signal the beginning of a more relaxed conversation. "The company needs to verify when the endorsement was made and when the loss happened. Nobody likes a dark cloud hanging over their head. The sooner I can make the sun shine, the better it is for everybody and I need to have your assistance to do that."

"I don't appreciate being put in this position. In all my years of writing policies, nobody ever put a tape recorder on my desk and asked me if I was telling the truth," he said.

"Certainly you can understand why it's important that there is no question in what you're telling us in case the insured is playing games with the date of loss. Memorializing this interview is an important step. Nobody can argue with what was asked or what was said." The logic of my statement didn't cool him off.

He was still hot under the collar that may not have been so tight two decades earlier. I shouldn't have been surprised when he said, "I'm gonna make a call and pull all my business with you guys. I am too old for this crap."

He might as well have knocked over a major piece and spit "checkmate" at me. This was a serious game he was playing.

Staring at my new employer's fire-mark on the wall, I imagined an empty blank rectangle of darkened wood. I couldn't blink now, literally and figuratively. I had to do something before this guy blew up.

"Give me to the end of the day before you make that call.

You owe it to yourself and the company. You have represented for them for how many years?"

We locked eyes again, but I could tell that he wanted to trust me. I conducted the interview professionally without pointing fingers at him or his staff for doing anything wrong or sloppy. There was nothing in the interview that gave me reason to doubt him either. I sent him that signal back.

"Longer than you've been on God's green earth young man." He was giving his ultimatum serious thought.

I tried to breathe easier and we sat some more.

"Okay," he finally said, "you'll call me before five, right?"

I finished my mug with a nod and set it on his desk as I rose. "Better get going, I'm burning daylight."

∾

I planned what should have been a pleasant late morning drive out of town to Bridgeport, NY, so that I could swing by the loss site on my way to the noon appointment with Mr. Insured. The agent's threat rang in my ears. He certainly raised the stakes. I wasn't about to call my boss with that news. I churned the newly-learned facts as I made my way through the farm country near Lake Oneida where the fields were already turned over, manured, and planted.

Building irrigation ponds was big business out here and Mr. Insured had the proper equipment to do it; dozers, excavators, backhoes, bobcats, and dump trucks. Some could be driven on country roads and others had to be towed on trailers. The insured's father started out as a farmer and, after some very nasty draughts, began building the ponds for himself and his fellow farmers. The agent continued to insure the son over the years and there was very little claims activity.

When I arrived at the scene, I walked the property. 35mm shots had been taken when the Bulldozer was being winched out of the pond and I used them for reference points. I could see the scarring of the pond embankments where the machine slid in and where its carcass was hauled out. I often stared at loss scenes and tried to imagine what had happened. What was this scene telling me? I could see that it was a savage battle to get the pond to give up its dead. Between the photos and the scene before me, the extra questions I would pose to the insured bubbled to the surface of my consciousness. This time, Sherlock Holmes would be proud of my Dr. Watson, as I scraped the mud from my shoes before getting back into the rental.

∾

It was a totally different vibe coming from Mr. Insured than the agent. Almost from the beginning, he was as slippery as the slime that sent his prized piece to the bottom of the pond. Even before I could turn the tape recorder on, he was fussing and fuming. He had a list of demands and questions for me and I had to keep referring him to the policy language invoking the 'cooperation clause'. He was throwing jabs to avoid going toe to toe with me. His hands were calloused and his face already showed the ruddy farmer's tan of a man used to spending long days outside in all kinds of weather, but his eyes were quick. He was also an astute businessman. We sat behind the military surplus desk next to the coal heater that warmed the converted barn housing his equipment. This was a man used to working long hours moving dirt, not reading the fine print of insurance policies, and his irritation, real or faked, was growing.

I could just see how this would play out as soon as I

drove off with the indignant insured melting the ear wax of his already pissed-off agent on the phone. If I didn't figure this claim out fast, the amount of the reserves set aside for this loss would pale in comparison with the threatened loss of revenue from the policy producer. This new venture of Special Investigations at the company would fade to black and I imagined yours truly being relegated to a phone cubicle explaining how deductibles worked on glass, towing and collision claims.

What a squeeze play! Be argumentative, don't submit to my questioning, wait for the end of the day and hope to outlast me. I needed to get something out of this whiner to work with. He had to give me some leads to roll on so that I could uncover the truth. It would be easy for me to roll over and soft pedal this case and, at the end of the day, give the agent a clean bill of health, tell him and the company that I couldn't find any evidence of wrongdoing and that I would recommend payment. Sure, I could get on the plane with my gifts for my wife and kids and pick up different dragon to slay tomorrow. The circumstances dictated that decision. Didn't they? Lose the battle, but live to fight another day. Right? I didn't have a choice when you really got down to it. Did I?

For years, those rationalizations would tempt me. It was a slippery slope, not much different than the one Mr. Insured had slid down in his bulldozer.

No, deep down I knew I had no choice. Tomorrow when I shave I had to stare at my own mug in the mirror. I'd have to look into my own eyes and see the coward who backed down. Had I ever backed down to bullies before? Did I ever look the other way? Did I ever take the easy way out? No, there wasn't really a choice here.

"..... I understand that you have not even okayed me

getting a replacement unit while the claim is being investigated, I-"

"Look," I said, "we can either do this now, as we agreed, or you can go to our lawyer's office in a couple of months, during your real busy season, and submit to an Examination Under Oath with a court reporter taking down every word. You can plan to be there the entire day and, oh by the way, you'll need to bring your tax returns, bank statements, P+Ls and receipts for the last three years." I stood up and closed my folio. "Your choice."

He motioned me to sit down and with a huff, the game of cat and rat continued.

As the tape rolled on, I went through my company-approved statement guide. Years of best practices went into developing the guide. However, In my years of taking recorded statements, I had learned to super-charge them with some additional open-ended questions that forced the respondent to offer time-narratives, rather than just answer a question with a couple of sentences. For the honest person, it usually meant retrieving the chronology from their memory banks; for the liars, it meant that they had to go off-script and make stuff up on the spot. Poker players watch their opponents closely for signs of what kind of hand they're holding or when they are bluffing. It's called watching for tells. What is your opponent *telling* you?

During a recorded statement or interview, the biggest tells were:

"Could you repeat the question?" Which he asked because he was stalling for time, followed by, "Why do you need to know that?", because he didn't like what was coming into his head for lies.

"Your claim didn't happen in a vacuum, you woke up that day and did other things before jumping on the bulldozer, so please tell me about your day up to the point where you started shoring up the embankment between the ponds."

There was definitely some funky things going on with this claim, but I kept my head down scribbling notes as I had since the beginning of the statement. I didn't want to give him any tells myself. As he fumbled through the explanation, one thing was for sure, the loss didn't happen on the day he claimed. It had to have happened prior to the policy endorsement date. I didn't doubt that it happened on a Saturday as he was working on his own ponds first before taking on orders for other farmer's. This equipment sat there idle all winter and you just didn't take off the canvass covers and turn the key. You had to wake up the unit with a battery charge, grease what needed greasing, and add fresh oil to the crankcase. He failed to say anything resembling any of that. I looked at the Saturday before the policy endorsement date on my day-timer and jotted that day down.

Mar 10th. I'd turn that card over last.

So we continued on with the statement until I hit him with, "Tell me about what you did to get your bulldozer out of the mud?"

"Could you repeat the question?"

"Tell me about what you did to get your bulldozer out of the pond?"

"Why do you need to know that?"

"Because all stories have a beginning, middle and an end- this is end. How did you get it out of the pond?"

He described calling the Tractor Trailer and Heavy Equipment Recovery Specialists in Watervliet, NY. He told me these guys had the equipment to haul tractor trailers that tumbled into ravines on the Thruway or transport massive quarry dump trucks that tipped over to repair shops. I pushed the photos on the desk between us in the tight space and he used them to explain how the unit was eventually winched out of the pond's death grasp.

"But, what are these marks over here?" I asked.

He screwed his face up in a puzzled look and said, "Oh, they tried to get it from a different angle the first time and it didn't work. They had to take it out by the ass end."

"Anybody else try to get the dozer out besides these guys with that wrecker?" I said tapping the photo.

"Nope."

Gotcha!

The statement proceeded to its almost conclusion with my heart rate lulling back to normal. Mr. Insured thought he was nearing the finish line and was starting to get his arrogance back when I zinged him.

"So when did you prep the dozer to get it ready for the season?"

"Whaddyamean?"

"What didn't you understand?"

I had looked up from my notes for the first time when I threw the zinger and was now watching his non-verbals and body language. He had that deer in the headlights look.

"I got all my equipment out and running the week before."

"What day was that?"

"Whadyamean?"

"What did I ask you?"

"You asked me what day did I get the dozer running?"

"What didn't you understand?"

"Saturday," he finally answered.

"Saturday, what date?" I asked.

Looking away from me to the girlie calendar above his desk, he said, "March 10th."

"Thank you," I replied.

He knew that I knew when the loss really happened and that I would figure it out somehow; he didn't know that I was racing the clock. Three hours to go before I was to call the agent. I knew from the tire tracks at the scene that at least two different recovery vehicles were used. One had dual rear axles, which was the big boy I saw in the photos, and then a smaller truck with a single set of smaller tires. I was betting that he tried to get the dozer out on the day it happened and when that failed, he hatched his plan to fool the agent and wait a week for the final reclamation to take place. It was one thing to give the agent a clean bill of health, but I had to shift his anger towards the insured for forcing the old guy to jump through all these hoops.

~

First things first. I was starved. The local diner had the three things this investigator needed: an all-day breakfast menu, clean toilets, and pay phones. Before sitting down, I dialed the wrecker service and left a message for the owner who was out on a run. His office girl wouldn't talk about the dozer with me and acted like I was an imposition on her time. Reminding her that the insurance company would be responsible for paying their bill helped her reconsider her attitude. I left my pager number for him and asked her if I could call him back around five. She said that was possible, acutely aware that I controlled the purse strings.

I tore through the Lumberjack Special while I chewed on the age old question. Does a tree make a sound when it falls down in the forest, if no one is there to hear it? Zen or not, it framed the real issue. In farm country, having your bulldozer disappear into the muddy morass of an irrigation pond is big news. Could I get someone to pin down when it happened? That was the $75,000 question. Could I get more than just hearsay? Could I get real proof that would stand up in court. The clock was ticking.

"Where you looking to go hon?"

I looked up from the *Mail it to you* map that was spread out on the table to see my waitress's name tag, (Were all diner waitresses named Dot, I wondered?) She had a fresh pot of coffee.

"To be honest, I was just trying to get my bearings. I'm in town today to try to find people that know about the bulldozer that went swimming in a pond just north of here in March."

She chuckled at the thought of a twelve ton piece of heavy equipment doing the butterfly stroke, while she poured my third refill.

"Maybe you ought to check with Jake over at Ed's garage. He knows most of the fellas around town that need their equipment fixed." She pointed to a spot on the map half way between town and the loss site.

"Thanks Dot. Where's the Post Office, Agway and Auto Parts stores?" I asked as I had not seen them when I made a beeline to the diner.

She pointed to each location and gave me a mini-briefing on who to talk to when I got there. You just have to love small-town America and 24-hour diners.

I thanked her twice with a big thank you and a tip that was half my bill. Refueled, I was ready to canvass the area for witnesses.

∾

"Jake ain't here," the pimply-faced gas pump jockey said.

Yelling over the heavy-metal music thumping that echoed in Ed's three-bay garage was not fun and the kid had no intention of turning it down while he was running the scrubber over the floors.

"He's out on a pick-up and won't be back for a while."

"Can I leave you my pager number for him to call me when he gets back?- It's about the bulldozer that slipped into an irrigation pond just up the road."

"Sure, you can leave it, but that doesn't mean he'll call you back."

"Why's that?" I asked.

"Jake's just that way." It was all the answer I would get, as he resumed scrubbing the floor.

Mary, the postmaster since forever, who knew everybody and their kin folks, acknowledged the well-wishes from Dot. She was more cheerful, but not anymore productive.

"I checked with the mail carrier that handles that route and he didn't hear anything about it or see anything while he was out there. None of the other carriers that were finishing their day can remember exactly when it happened. Too much time has gone by," she said.

She had gone back to talk to her mail carriers alone and as much as I wanted to ask the questions and see their reactions, it was still a government facility and I wasn't allowed back where they sorted the mail. I had worked with US Postal Inspectors before and it would have been nice if one magically appeared at that moment out in the boonies. He or she could just stroll on back there with me and we do the questioning ourselves.

I methodically clicked off my to-do list each of the adjoining properties surrounding the irrigation pond. Knocking on doors and pounding the pavement was not glamorous, but very effective when asking about something as unique as your neighbor losing a bulldozer to Mother Nature. The witness-canvass did not produce the correct date. His neighbors had all heard about it and tried to remember when they heard about it. I asked them where they were or what they were doing when they heard about it. Bridge night? Bowling league? Bible Study? Choir practice? Movie night? Anything to tie down a specific date when they heard the news. If they had heard the about the bad fortune before the claimed date of loss and could corroborate the date they heard about it, though other means, I could learn who knew about it firsthand.

The Agway dealer knew the insured well and said that he was a good customer. He had heard from the insured about the tragic loss and said that it happened on the day for which the insured was making the claim.

"I have no reason to doubt him. He and his father have been customers of mine for over 50 years."

"Besides him telling you when it happened, do you have anything else to show that it happened that day?" I asked.

"I'm sure he's being straight with you," was his response in the form of an answer.

On the way to the Auto Parts store, I spotted a barber shop and it not being a Monday, I walked in and saw the barber lathering hot shaving cream on the neck of an old-timer in overalls, while two other gents of similar age waited. For an eight dollar haircut, you got your neck shaved and your eye brows and nose hairs trimmed. He steadily scraped the lather off with an ivory handled straight-edged razor without making any eye-contact with me.

"We all laughed when we heard it. You did what? How could you have let that happen?" He related to me how they all had made so much fun at Mr. Insured's expense. This is where he went for his regular haircut. We all looked at the local Farmer and Mechanic's bank calendar on the wall and they couldn't be sure what day the land mover pretended to be a submarine.

The Auto Parts store was the last stop. It was now past 4PM and the owner wanted to close his drawer and make like a bunny and hop on out of there. He didn't know when the loss happened, but like everybody else in the bustling burg of Bridgeport, NY, he had heard about it.

"It's really important to me for you to check your receipts and see when he bought the grease, oil, and filters," I said. Mr. Insured had supplied this store as the source.

"The bookkeeper got all the paperwork for quarterlies, I am sorry," he said.

Was he trying to get me to leave? Had he been given a heads up to be on the look out for me? I pressed him.

"Give me the bookkeeper's address and we can call from here and you can pave the way so that I look at them there. It will only take a minute. I can't sign off on the guy's claim until I verify them."

"Hold on." With that, he disappeared into the supply room.

I stood there and thought about where I was in the investigation. In less than an hour, I had to call the agent. I could clear him of any suspected wrongdoing, but couldn't pin anything on his client. It wasn't in the local paper as an item of interest. People knew about it, but enough time had elapsed that nobody could be sure of the date that they heard about it. I still had an outstanding call with the wrecker service and I would call them before I called the agent. This was my last stop.

The owner returned with a cigar box of receipts. Turns out that the bookkeeper hadn't picked them up yet, or so he said. We went through the numbered receipts until we got to March 9th. There were Mr. Insured's purchases of the grease, oil, and filters for his heavy equipment. So he did get them 8 days before the loss, but what did that prove? I started to put the receipts back in the box and apologized for taking the shop owner's time when I saw the next slips for March 10th. There was another slip for Mr Insured.

"What's this for?" I ask.

His eyes widened in recognition, but then he tried being nonchalant. "Nothing really- just some chocks to keep your tires from rolling when you're working on your brakes."

"What size tires are they for?"

"Whaddyamean?"

"Are they for passenger car tires or bigger truck tires?"

"Why do you need to know that?"

Again the stalling tactic, what did it matter to him what size they were?

"Why do you ask?" I ask.

"I don't understand why that is important to you."

"Look you're in a hurry to close up shop, get the hell out of here, and go home. Why do you want me to explain why an insurance investigator is asking you what size the chocks are? Isn't just easier to tell me?"

He didn't want to lie to me, but he didn't want to tell me the answer I now suspected.

"They are for trucks, they are heavy duty."

"Did he say why he needed them?"

"I don't remember, probably had to do with working on his trucks."

"Do you remember when he bought them?"

"It says it right there." He pointed indignantly to the date.

"No, I mean what time of day did he come in to buy them."

"Listen, I've showed you the receipts you asked me about, I'm done-."

"Hold on a second, there's an easier way." I pulled the cigar box back in our little tug of war.

It took me less than a minute to put the purchase between three and four that fateful Saturday afternoon based upon the times printed out on the cash register tapes affixed to the credit card sales. I made a point of putting my initials and today's date on the important ones.

"Thank you." I said as I noted that in my files. "Don't lose these receipts or you'll get a subpoena to spend a day in court explaining why you don't have them after we both saw them and I just initialed and dated them in front of you."

After I slammed the door to my rental (after all, it was a rental), I peeled out of his driveway; the same driveway that I imagined a just as pissed-off, but muddy, Mr. Insured pulled into late in the afternoon of the Saturday in question. I suspected he had to buy chocks so the truck trying to winch out his dozer wouldn't keep sliding into the pond as well. The Auto Parts store owner knew damn well what happened that day and he was lying to me and I couldn't prove it.

I had to calm down and reassess. I had about a half-hour to work on this case before calling the wrecker driver and the agent. My mind was whirling with emotions from the long day, the import of the agent's threat, and the store-owner playing games with me in the final minutes. I had run out of leads. This was frustrating. I knew the guy was dirty, but I couldn't prove it. I started to visualize the dreaded conversation with the agent, but something clicked, as I passed the VFW on the left side of the road back to the airport. What was that? What did I see? I u-turned and pulled into the gravel lot next to the 105mm Howitzer and marble stone lined flag pole stand. To the other side of my rental sat the object my subconscious mind observed while I was doing my woe-is-me routine. There were several pick-up trucks and a rusty tow truck from Ed's Garage. The tow truck had a winch on it. My pulse quickened, as I walked past the truck and confirmed two very muddy heavy-duty chocks wrapped with a bungee cord around the tool chest.

It didn't take me long to slide up next to Jake. His stool was in front of the flickering TV mounted over the bar. Flags, Military Unit patches, maps, bayonets, a German Luger, photos of groups and individuals in the different branch of service uniforms festooned the grease and nicotine coating the lime-green walls. There was the obligatory dartboard, billiard table and jukebox. He was staring dull-eyed with an overturned shot glass, crowded ashtray of Pall Malls, and half-empty draft of Genesee Cream Ale arrayed in front of him. The bartender was cleaning glasses halfway between him and the TV. Both their eyes were glued to the skimpily-clad game-show girl showing off the prize behind door number three. With Jake, it looked like his glass was always half-empty and that he desperately wanted to be in that vacation spot with that young pretty thing.

I ordered a ginger ale, took a sip, and began shaking my head. "I betcha he didn't even pay you, Jake," I said.

He looked over at me and said, "who? What are you talking about?"

I didn't take my eyes off the tube. "Mr. Big Shot. The guy who gets his bulldozer stuck in the pond and gets mad at you because your tow truck didn't have the muscle to yank it out."

"Oh him, yeah he's a world-class pain in the butt. I ain't

gonna see a dime from him." I almost burned out my winch trying to get that thing outta there. It wasn't going anywhere and he got mad at me. The dumb-ass. I didn't drive it into the pond."

I slid my card onto the glass covered bar between the beer suds, cigarette ashes, and whiskey drippings.

"I know I could get you paid, if I knew the date that you went on that call." Still not making eye-contact, I began studying the top shelf liquor.

He held my card up to the light to see it better. The lighting was just a little better than your average last chance shot and beer dive bar, but good enough to read. I could tell that he was guarded by my approach, a stranger in a suit and tie at the VFW. He was mulling things over in his mind. The country-western music faded from the juke box about the time he said, "Edna and I were on the way to her sister's kid's birthday party when I got the call. Since it was on the way, we jumped in the truck and headed over.

"Uh-huh." I turned to look at him. "What happened next?"

"Well, by the time we got there, he had it stuck in there pretty good. It wasn't underwater yet. He tried easing it out but each time he tried backing up the embankment, it slid a little lower. He figured if I was winching it, while he was backing out, he'd be able to get her out. It wasn't a bad idea until he started to pull my truck in with him. I yelled for him to stop and instead he pushed his treads faster. I had to release him or he would have pulled my truck in. When I did, his treads kept spinning, and he slid back down even deeper."

"That's when he ran to the Auto Parts Store to get the chocks, right?" Now I wished I had taken those receipts when I had the chance.

He nodded, "Edna took some pictures with her VCR camera that she was taking to her nephew's birthday party, while we waited. It started to get late and she was really giving it to me while we sat there and watched it sink deeper."

"Which day was that?

"Same day as the day her nephew was born, nine years ago- March 10th."

"You sure?"

~

"That Son of a Bitch!" He roared for the fifth time as I told him the whole story from the airport gate area with thirty minutes to go before my departure. I had called him earlier from the VFW while Jake used the bathroom and told him that I had really good news, and that I would call just before I took off. Keeping somebody in suspense like that is sometimes a good thing.

"So I followed Jake back to his house and Edna reluctantly gave me the tape of her Nephew's ninth birthday party after we watched it. I had to promise her that I'd make a copy of it and send her back the copy. She had both the bulldozer and the party on the same VCR cassette and yes, the date stamp clearly showed March 10th. Your boy definitely had the loss before he asked you to endorse the equipment onto the policy. I told Jake we'd pay his bill for the work that day. I told the wrecker guy that we would pay him too. Your policyholder had kept that wrecker guy in the dark, like he did you. We'll need his cooperation if your client decides to fight this."

"You send his Claims Withdrawal to me, you won't have any problem with him. He'll sign it and be thankful that this isn't going to my friend over at the State Police barracks. I am dropping him like a hot potato the minute he signs it. I'll make sure no agent in a hundred mile radius will touch that son of a bitch."

It was about that time that I accidentally pressed the talk button on my daughter's doll in the bag of goodies for my family, "Mama".

"What's that?" he asked.

"Just a talking doll for my daughter. I always get them gifts when I travel."

So that started us talking about family a little bit, I was from the Philly area, met my wife of twelve years at college and that I have two children; an eight year old son, who was in cub scouts and played soccer and a two year old daughter that thankfully wasn't going through the terrible twos and just recently started wearing big girl underwear. Since we're great buddies now, I told him how I'd been a cop and a claims manager and used those combination punches to knock out quite a few fraudsters before coming to work for the company. He told me that he was a great-grand father three times over and was working now just to keep out of his wife's hair.

Before ringing off, he promised to put a good word in for me with the Sales side of my new organization. That would be nice, but not necessary, I told him. My newest friend insisted. I demurred.

The fatigue of the day finally hit me, just as they announced it was time to say goodbye to 'Cuse. I gulped the last dregs of my airport coffee before bracing for the not-quite fresh spring air out to the tarmac. God, I hate the smell of jet fuel in the evening.

LONELY NIGHTS

G reeeeeeen. Yellow. Reeeeed. In the background, behind the traffic light, a Blue and Mustard-colored Sunoco sign revolves oh so slowly.

Greeeeeeen, Yellow Reeeeed. I am doing breathing exercises in time with the light sequences, pausing on Yellow.

0300 hours, I am working alone on the graveyard shift as patrol car 46-3. My partner called in sick. I am making up this game to keep awake.

Greeeeeen, Yellow. Reeee-Exhale. I spot a beat up black Dodge Polara barreling through the red light. Finally, something to do.

I call in to dispatch I am stopping the car with the single white male occupant. My locus is a half mile north of the town's main intersection of Rte. 202 and Rte. 73 on Dekalb Pike which was named after a revolutionary war hero. Two miles west is some of the best Pennsylvania farmland, now being used for sod farms to meet the needs of the growing suburbs. Yet, I'm standing just 10 miles from the North Philadelphia to the east, the worst crime-ridden section in the City of Brotherly Love. This guy is coming from the south with blue alpha-numerics on a white-faced Virginia license plate sporting a current 1976 registration sticker.

As I collect my hat and oversized flashlight, I always follow procedure. At twenty-one, I am a newly-minted rookie on this suburban police force, just three months out of the academy. I know that next to domestic disturbances, a car stop has the highest rate of police killings. I am out here alone. No backup.

My cruiser's swivel searchlight is aimed on the driver's side view mirror and the back of driver's body, lighting up the inside of the car like daylight that, unfortunately, is still a couple hours away on this sultry summer night.

Sitting on the broken down bench seat of the town's oldest Plymouth Gran Fury police interceptor had shifted the business parts of my uniform into uncomfortable positions. I adjust my Sam Browne belt, which holds my holster and handcuffs over my pants belt. The Second Chance bullet proof vest my mother bought me when I graduated from the police academy was pinching my chest as I make my way to the stopped vehicle. There are no other cars or street lights on this lonely stretch of asphalt. It is dead quiet.

A lefty, I unsnap my holster and grip the handle of my department issued .38 caliber police chief special four inch revolver. There are no routine traffic stops, the instructors had pointed out during role play in the outdoor classes.

My Chief has told me, this bi-Centennial year, to be courteous to out of staters as they are bringing tourist dollars to the Greater Delaware Valley. My flashlight sweeps the back seat clean and fixates on the man's hands as I ask him for his driver's license, vehicle registration and proof of insurance. The man turns them over in quick order. There is no smell of alcohol or pot coming from the interior. I tell the man about the stop light and the speeding. The man politely nods in resignation, but doesn't say anything. *You got me.*

I radio in the 10-28, which is a records check, to county dispatch with his Driver's License and Registration info and am told that our terminal to NCIC (The National Crime Information Center) mainframe computer is down and can't be checked for out of state suspensions, wants, or warrants right now. *Wonderful.*

I re-approach the car and caution the man to drive more carefully through the Keystone state. The man visibly relaxes and thanks me for giving him a break and drives off while I log in the warning with dispatch. I lead the department in both tickets and warnings. Car stops in my blossoming career have yielded some good busts. Each one is different but some can be routine like this warning. I clear the scene with dispatch and resume patrol; anything to relieve the boredom.

I do a quick zip around the town's retail stores and businesses and shake doors for the signs of break-ins. I drive by the other Sunoco station in town where I had worked pumping gas just five years earlier before going to college It was there, that I poured premium into the thirsty gas tanks of the town's police cars while they filled me with cop stories. When they got a hot call and peeled out with lights and sirens, I stood there with my dripping squeegee and was hooked. I knew what I wanted to be when I grew up.

I'm back at the main intersection now. The hours are dragging by. Greeeen. Yellow. Reeeeed. The monotony and the false dawn are settling on me like the dew forming on my black and white cruiser. One more hour to until shift change. I am thinking about having a bowl of cereal with my cute girlfriend, before she heads off for work. Then, I will settle down with a Scotch and Captain Kangaroo before drifting off to sleep.

Greeeen. Yell- The Motorola radio erupts, "46-3!" "46-3!" "Do you still have Virginia plate AZC-746 stopped?" There is an urgency in the dispatch supervisor's voice.

I lurch into a ramrod straight position and reply, "46-3, Negative. Advised County that subject was given a warning and released over three hours ago." *What the hell?*

I am still clearing the cobwebs from my brain when she says, "46-3 be advised that subject is wanted by Richmond, Virginia PD for the shooting of a police officer, go back to station and await further instructions."

DOUBLE TROUBLE

"You know damn well that I wanted to take a recorded statement. We scheduled this time and this place to do it." The micro-cassette recorder sat impotently on the table in front of me. He had been jerking me around for close to a half-hour and I was losing my patience.

"I don't remember ever saying that I was going to sit here and have you grill me. You know the fine print of insurance policies and I am afraid to say something that will give you the reason to deny my claim," Mr. Blowhard said. Dressed in a blue blazer over an open-collared white button-down pressed shirt, chinos and deck shoes with no socks, he was every bit the part of the put-off, well-to-do yachtsman.

"From now on, we will do everything in writing. If I don't get a recorded statement now, the next step will be an Examination Under Oath and a production of documents, including your financial statements for the last three years," I said. This was my last shot to get something productive out of a three hour trek that started before dawn and into a blinding sun and metro rush hour before arriving at the marine surveyor's offices on Boston's South Shore.

"Is this normal? I paid my premium. My boat is missing. I reported it right away to the agent. The adjustor already talked to me. You tried to trick me and now you are threatening me with a lawyer. I am not sure that you are treating me fairly."

"You have to cooperate with the investigation of this claim. I am the investigator. There are questions that need to be answered. You have an obligation to answer them."

"Not now and not with you pal." With that parting shot, he got up and walked out of the conference room.

I was fuming, this was his plan all along. He came today to size me up and try to find out why a Special Investigator had been assigned to his missing boat claim. He was fishing and I wouldn't bite. The policy said he had to cooperate, but nowhere did it say I had to tell him why I was investigating his claim, and that's what we had been going round and round on. He must have known that I couldn't deny his claim for failing to give me a recorded statement.

The marine surveyor hustled into the conference room as soon as Mr. Blowhard motored out leaving me bobbing in his wake.

"That didn't sound good," he said. Henry has been surveying watercraft since his discharge from the navy after Korea. He could tell you the value of a boat and, as importantly, how much it would cost to repair one that was damaged or replace one that was stolen by just looking at a good set of photos.

I stared out into the marina next to his offices. Yachts, power boats, cigar boats, sail boats; all kinds of pleasure craft were in the water or up on stilts. The pilings acted as sentinel stands for the seagulls to keep watch on. They were giving me a one-eye stare and judging me now on what a lousy job I did of casting a net around this insured.

"Henry, that sailor boy just played me," I said. "He wanted to see if the coast was clear."

"What did he say about buying it for salvage?" Henry asked.

"Nothing, we didn't even get that far. He didn't carry in any paperwork either. That was my first clue that I wasn't going fishing with him."

Henry just shook his head. "Doesn't make sense that he'd come all this way not to give you a statement."

"Sure it does. Somehow, he knew that I am not part of the normal claims process and when it became obvious that I was going to ask lots of questions, he walked, but not without trying to get something out of me first."

"He's hiding something," Henry said.

"Yeah, but what?" I said. It was Henry who first suspected something was amiss a month ago, when he was assigned by my company's yacht claims manager to work up a replacement value for the missing boat. Turns out that Henry had seen the boat last year, right after Hurricane Bob. Its starboard side was smashed into matchsticks when Bob roared up the coast all the way to Canada, hitting all the marinas on the East Coast like a little kid splashing around in a bath tub. The yacht manager, in turn, made a referral to me when he learned that the agent had not seen the boat before putting it on the policy. Then the red flags really went up when its inspection was delayed twice by Mr. Blowhard, before the boat mysteriously disappeared.

We both looked out at the gorgeous day unfolding, but little did we know about the next storm that was brewing just beyond the horizon.

～

He revved the engine and blared the horn. It was going to be close. The mad Slav was bearing down on the jay-walker that pretended not to see his bright Yellow Cab. The pedestrian jumped out of the way with inches to spare as he blurred past my passenger window.

"They move." the Slav said curtly.

The thrill ride up North Calvert Street from BWI through the Inner Harbor of Baltimore, Balmer to the locals, couldn't take my mind off why I had been summoned to my employer's home office on the North side of town. It was all about that sailboat and how Mr. Blowhard was trying to turn the tables on me. Baltimore was a busy seaport. Cargo ships, Supertankers and the gigantic cranes hovering over the water reminded me of Philadelphia or Boston with just as rich real history. It was from this very harbor that Francis Scott Key penned our National Anthem.

I worried, even though my boss assured me, that I wasn't being called on the carpet and that they would come to my office in my home if they were going to fire me. I had jumped on a USAir direct from New Haven to Balmer to brief the president himself of the billion dollar insurance company I worked for. I was holding up the payment on this yacht claim. Normally, a claim investigation or even a denial of payment would not merit a meeting with a president. This was unheard of, but the boat owner had raised the stakes. He seriously upped the ante and I wasn't about to fold my hand. Being a fairly good poker player, I recognized the bluff, but now I was being told that it wasn't my pile of chips that I was playing with anymore. The company needed to see my hand.

I was ushered into the finely appointed board room overlooking the Balmer City skyline and Inner Harbor. The president gave me a nod from the head of the long table opposite me. The furniture, all deep colored woods, was made with the precise hand-crafting of a pre-industrial time. The artwork depicted fox hunting scenes renowned for the area. *Who was the fox today?*, I wondered. The scenes of rolling horse farms harkened back to that time between our founding as a country and the war to prove once and for all that we were truly United States. Flanking us along the Mahogany table were the claims guys on one side and the marketing suits on the other. Too many to play poker and too many to make the decision, as far as I was concerned.

Flanking the president furthest from me, were the vice-presidents of Marketing and Claims staring at each other. Next, the Marine or Yacht program marketing manager sat across from the Yacht claims manager and lastly, the Marine underwriter was positioned across from my boss, the director of Special Investigations or SIU.

The president and I could see each other's reflection in the table top and I could tell he was sizing me up. I was told that he was a maverick, a real firebrand with a quick temper. My reputation as a "Top Gun" and a straight shooter earned me a seat at this shindig. Maybe, if we stared long enough at each other's reflections, we might get a glimpse inside.

"This is a grave matter. Never before in the history of the company have we ever been faced with such a threat to our position in the industry. Our carefully designed marketing program to boat owners is one of trust and indemnity." The head honcho from marketing began. He fired the first shot across our bow.

As if on cue, the Marketing manager continued. "The Yacht program is the most successful program we have. It gives us warm relationships with wealthy individuals, businesses, and corporations. This is a demographic that we don't want to lose."

The underwriter looked up from his spreadsheets and agreed. "The combined-loss ratio for this line of business is the lowest by a far margin." This was insurancese for saying that although the program wasn't making a lot of money, it had the highest profit margin.

But then, the eight hundred pound gorilla was introduced to the room when the Marketing Veep said, "Our parent company could easily sell this piece of business off-it's our flagship." There it was finally out on the table.

The conversation just shifted from a not-so-simple boat claim, to the end of their careers. The recent history was pretty straight-forward. A foreign multi-national had bought the company and installed this president to turn it around and make it profitable. If we couldn't do better than the fixed rate of return from thirty-year Treasury notes, the company would be broken up and sold. The individual parts would fetch more then what they paid for the sum. The pressure to produce was on. This old-line venerable carrier was under assault on several fronts. They were slow to catch up with automation. Dumb CRT terminals still fed data to a balky mainframe for overnight batch processing. Claim payments went out from one central location, the next day.

Direct Writers like GEICO and Progressive were cutting out the middleman, the agents, with brutal efficiencies. They were killing the old school agency system with saturation marketing. It seemed the independent agency system with hefty commissions was going the way of dinosaurs. My employer was slow to get on board with SIU and was being targeted by professional fraudsters. We were one of the last companies to shove off with a bonafide SIU program. It hadn't been smooth sailing and now our actions, more appropriately mine, were being called into question.

A silence fell over the room, a long uncomfortable silence; The kind of silence that begged me to say something. Anything.

"Since when do we negotiate with terrorists?" I asked. Before anyone could answer, I added, "This is a shake-down, pure and simple."

Defending the honor of the boat owner he never met or talked to, the Marketing manager shot back. "Your attitude, Mr. Hoda, is precisely why he has requested that you be removed from this claim."

"I've known John for twelve years and he has worked dozens of cases with serious criminal implications and never once did his professionalism or character come into question. I wouldn't want anybody else on this case. Besides, I thought we could all talk frankly here." My boss delivered his own volley.

Emboldened, the Yacht claims manager zinged the Marketing manager. "Understand that all of this came about because the agent didn't inspect the Marlow-Hunter 37 before putting it on the policy. By the time underwriting scheduled the marine surveyor to inspect it, it was gone. All we have is this one photo. But what made me refer this claim to SIU, was the fact that, after Hurricane Bob turned hundreds of boats into matchsticks, the same surveyor had inspected - this same Marlow-Hunter , deemed it a total loss and later sold it to the policyholder for salvage. How did this vessel rise up from the graveyard and become seaworthy? That's what I want to know."

Following his lead I added, "That was exactly the tact I took when I scheduled a meeting with the insured. He insisted on a time, early in the morning, at the surveyor's office on the South Shore of Boston. I was crystal clear that I wanted to take his recorded statement. He knew I was driving up from New Haven before dawn." I was now talking directly to the president. Everyone else could wait their turn. I was telling a story.

"So I schlep up there with the sun in my eyes the whole way and this joker gets cold feet, telling me that I never told him I wanted to take his statement. The whole time he is trying to wheedle information out of me about the claim's process, how much I knew and what I was planning to do. He came to the meeting empty-handed even after I told him that I needed to review all his purchase invoices and repairs and maintenance logs. He didn't produce any documentation whatsoever and wasn't going to talk to me on tape. He was on a fishing expedition and when he realized that I was the real deal, he wasn't going to sit there and watch me filet him. I was pissed, but I didn't show it. I quietly told him that our next meeting would be when he submitted to our attorneys examining him under oath and that he would be required to produce what I had originally asked for plus all his financials for the last three years."

Those at the table knew the next step after that would be to mail him a formal proof of loss. Both the Examination Under Oath and the Proof of Loss could be required under the terms and conditions of his yacht policy. If he didn't comply, we could deny his claim for lack of cooperation. Ironclad defenses. With no lien holder on the vessel, he would be out for everything that he put into it.

"I heard a different account of how that meeting went down from the agent." the Marketing manager said. I decided then and there that he was the designated hatchet man for this meeting.

Keeping my eyes on the president, I continued, without taking the bait. "So I went ahead and contacted one of the best insurance fraud attorneys that I know, who just so happens to practice in the Commonwealth of Massachusetts.

"What happened next?" The president asked a simple question that cut through all their posturing. How refreshing.

"We raised the ante and scheduled the Examination Under Oath of not only him but also his wife who was also named on the policy. That's when he called our raise and upped the ante with that letter."

The letter I was referring to was the top sheet of the packet brought in by each of the suits. I was familiar enough with the contents to have it committed to memory. Mr. Blowhard was threatening to take out a double page ad in the most widely read boating magazine, inviting other plaintiffs to join him in a class action suit against the company if they felt their boat claims were not paid promptly or in full. Talk about throwing chum into the shark pool. That move caught everyone by surprise.

Fingering the piece of paper like it was kryptonite, the Marketing Veep said, "We can't afford this negative publicity even if it is groundless and without merit." Dropping it on the table, he added. "It's better to make a business decision and quietly settle this case."

The argument was a good one. Pay an $80,000 claim and save possibly untold hundreds of thousands of premium dollars from being lost thanks to the negative press.

The conversation turned to how the advertisement could have a snow-ball effect. They did not have an apparatus in place to deal with the adverse publicity. Agents would drop them. The demographic, we so coveted, would quietly not renew or expand their coverages. The gloom and doom continued. There was lots of cross-talk. The president and I just listened. From time to time he would look at me. I didn't flinch. *Business Decision* was just a euphemism for looking the other way. I didn't do it as a cop, I didn't do it in the fifteen years since I left the PD and I wasn't going for it now.

Above the din, the top dog asked, "what do you think? Will he do it?" He was staring at me.

All eyes were on me now. Not just the people in the room assembled, but my wife and kids back home, the banker who held my mortgage, the church where we tithed, the car loan company. I took a deep breath. I had met the boat owner only once and talked to him on the phone briefly to set up that meeting. I didn't have a crystal ball, but I had sparred with him enough to get a sense of who I was dealing with.

"No sir, he's bluffing. He just wants money. Causing us all kinds of pain will not put a dollar in his pocket. He'd be smart to walk away now, but his Achilles heel is that he thinks he's smarter than all of us."

Nobody in the room was going to admit to that.

That message got through loud and clear to the president. "Okay", looking back and forth at his Veeps, "tell the agent that we are not responding to this guy's threat and that we expect him to comply with the terms and conditions of his policy in making the claim." Looking at me with a hard stare, "Hoda, you've got 60 days after that proof of loss is filed to finish your investigation, is that clear?"

"Yes sir."

∾

"He didn't send us anything," our lawyer said. We met to go over any documents that may have arrived by next-day delivery that morning.

"Playing head games again," I said.

"No policy provision says he has to send his documentation in ahead of his EUO."

We were early for the meeting with the insured. The transcriptionist set up her equipment at our end of the table. This room was used by out of town lawyers for depositions or examinations under oath (EUO) at the old Essex County Courthouse.. It was a nice day, clear, warm and sunny. It was a shame that I had to sit inside, head down taking notes. The two earlier meeting dates had been postponed; most recently because his wife claimed to be sick and on the first occasion when the boat owner said he had trouble getting all the requested documents together in time. He was not represented by a lawyer and they would attend by themselves. Not that it would matter much. Other than objecting to form or relevancy of the questioning, a lawyer would still have to sit there and watch his or her client answer the questions. That's how it worked with an EUO. My job was to make sure that amongst all the bluster and posturing, the questions would be answered to my lawyer's satisfaction. I also listened to the language used by the policyholder to present his claim under oath.

Since graduating with a B.S. in Criminology in 1975, eighteen years earlier, I had made the art and science of interviewing my specialty. First was the Reid Technique, then Investigative Discourse Analysis and just lately the basic and advanced schooling of Avinoam Sapir, an Israeli polygraph specialist at the Laboratory of Scientific Interrogation in the SCAN technique. These classes were not about learning parlor tricks. Watching body language, listening to the language people used to talk about an event and dissecting written or transcribed statements became a potent tool in my arsenal. It was amazing stuff really. I learned that people used different language in recalling an event from memory than if they were making it up. I was beginning to see the forest from the trees. Just a simple change in pronouns or ending a statement with "that's about it" were only two cues of many to press the interview into great depth. Day in and day out, I was practicing better interview techniques and on long rides in the car, I would play back recorded statements to grade myself.

My thoughts were interrupted when Mr. Blowhard walked into the room and took one look at me.

"I don't want him here."

"Good morning sir, do you have the requested-for information pursuant to the terms and conditions of your policy," my lawyer replied.

"I said that I don't want that guy in the room. You didn't say that he would be here." He hadn't sat down yet and was trying to establish control.

"Thank you for your response, but could you please answer my question. Have you brought the information that we requested?" My lawyer didn't blink.

"You don't get it. I'm not saying anything, until he leaves the room."

"I'll ask the transcriptionist to start transcribing right now. I want to have this conversation recorded. If you decide to leave this room now, the company will consider you to be in breach of the policy conditions and I will recommend that they deny your claim for failure to cooperate. Mr. Hoda will not talk to you, he will only address me during this session. I will be asking all the questions. " With that my lawyer launched into the preamble and the transcriptionist began working the keys.

He stood there undecided as my lawyer finished the preamble, " and let the record reflect that the policyholder is present. Would you please have a seat and spell your name for the record."

We sat there and waited. The transcriptionist's fingers were poised over the keys.

He tried to even up the odds and now he was forced to fish or cut bait.

I envisioned opening a copy of *Boaters World* to the staple pages in a couple of months and seeing a nice glossy two-page four-color advertisement inviting all kinds of whoop-ass on my soon to be ex-employer. Of course, the nice people in the unemployment line would be wondering why I was reading about yachts when I was trying to collect.

"Yeah, if he says one word to me, I am out of here, you got that." He sat down with a huff and tossed an overstuffed manila envelope of papers on the desk.

I smiled. I didn't have to say a damn thing. I didn't have to think of how to formulate questions, what sequence to put them in or even how to phrase them, I just had to listen and pass notes to my lawyer who had turned the switch on and became the steely-eyed professional.

"- and I consider this harassment. I paid my premium and reported a legitimate loss. I have not been paid a dime and have not had the pleasure of my boat through all of the boating season and you're telling me you want more information. When will this nit-picking end."

By the time he started this line of rehearsed complaining, we'd been at it for over three hours. Each document was discussed in detail and most were marked as exhibits. There were numerous times when I passed a note. *He didn't answer your question.* The first few times, my lawyer would look at his notes, pause and ask the transcriptionist to read back the responses. Very quickly, he learned to state. "Thank you for your response, but my question was---".

Talk about a worm squirming on the hook. There were times when the insured would launch into some long-winded explanation and my lawyer would hold his pen in mid-air eye-closed and listen until the amateur sailor would have no more wind in his sail. Then the lawyer would repeat, "Thank you for your response, but my question was----"

I counted him doing this four times in a row when he asked about the insured's movements in the 24-hour period prior to when the insured discovered his boat missing from a mooring at the marina. Our boy wasn't prepared for that question and was floundering. He bought a salvage piece at auction and contracted with a "friend in the business" to restore it. The friend wanted to be paid cash under the table which the insured agreed to and then refused to produce a receipt. The friend didn't want to pay taxes on the income for his labor. The stammering continued when we asked him where and how often he visited his boat during the re-build. He gave us the name of the supplier of some of the materials as he paid for them directly and had gotten receipts. He was vague on details and said that his friend had moved and disconnected his telephone line after their last argument. So there we were. No one else rode with him before he reported his boat missing. He could not produce any receipts for overnight stays at marinas around Boston or Cape Cod. Nobody else could put him in that boat from the time it was allegedly repaired until it was mysteriously stolen. He hadn't enough time on the water to really take her out on a shakedown cruise, we were told.

The insured showed us large cash withdrawals from his checking account that became his representations of how much and when he paid his friend. They got the boat into the water. He talked about their maiden voyage with ease and enthusiasm. How did he handle the mainsail and the jib? What kind of knots did he use for the ropes? What instruments did he have on the bridge? I didn't know a jib from a jab until earlier in the week when I had the marine surveyor educate me about boating for an hour. I still thought of a boat as a hole in the water that you poured money into. I could never understand how you could spend that much money on a short-season hobby in New England. Talking to the surveyor and now to the insured about sailing, you thought that if God made anything better, God kept it in heaven.

The Lawyer paused and this was my cue to look up for the one-two punch of questions that were about to follow. I had been surreptitiously watching our boy's mannerisms while answering questions to that point and now I wanted to see his reactions to these two questions.

"What should happen to the person that made your boat disappear?"

Now if it was my $80,000 boat that got stolen I would use every pirate movie phrase from walking the plank to getting keel-hauled as to the fate of the person that made off with my pride and joy. Instead I heard;

"Could you repeat the question?" He clearly understood the hundred other questions that day.

"What should happen to the person that made your boat disappear?

Silence, then slowly. "Well, he should be made to give it back."

"Will you assist in the prosecution of the person responsible and assist in obtaining restitution for any expenditures made by the company resulting from this claim?"

"I guess."

"Could you answer yes or no?"

"Yes."

"Thank you for your time here today. There is still the matter of certain documents that we asked for that you did not bring today. This EUO is not concluded until we have possession of them and your notarized signature agreeing with what you said today." The attorney went on to list on the record the documents that we still needed. I sat back and stared at the insured for the first time all day. Slumped over, sullen with arms and hands below the table, I had seen that posture many times before. This was a simple examination under oath, not an interrogation. No trickery or half-truths, no confrontations to forcefully overcome objections, no softer themes of why he decided to commit an insurance fraud. This was just skillful questioning with a few zingers thrown in.

Exhausted, he made the same tired arguments why his claim should be paid and then demanded to sit in while his wife was examined. Usually, we would ask that only one person would be permitted to in the room at a time. We didn't want him to poison the well. We didn't object because we had the sense that she would not have anything substantive to offer and we were right. He sat there while she told us that she had never been on the boat, never seen the boat in any stage of repair and that she didn't know anything about their finances as he handled all of their money. She was a dental assistant working full-time. They had no kids. We asked her about when his boating hobby started and what kind of boats he owned previously to this ocean-going single mast sail boat. It was clearly a hobby that she was not a part of. In their life together, there were many things that she was not a part of. She had the steady income and benefits. She stayed home and worked and he did this or that and played on weekends.

His records were on the table and she confirmed that he bounced around sales jobs and then into multi-level marketing. His earnings over the past three years were dependent on where you were looking. His reported earnings to the IRS and Massachusetts were just-above the poverty line, yet you saw these large swings of cash in and out of his checkbook. Seeing his reported finances splayed out in front of his wife became increasingly difficult to him and her when we pointed out how much cash was coming in and going out. She was clueless but was starting to get the picture. Ms Frugality meet Mr. Big-Spender, but not on her. Our examination was coming to a close, but we got the queasy sense that her questioning of him would continue well into their evening, behind closed doors with the drapes tightly drawn.

You had to feel sorry for her, but not for Mr. Blowhard. He was a player and he was trying to play us all. This day it caught up to him. It may be the first time in his recent life that somebody held him accountable for his actions.

∾

We sat outside in the beautiful sunshine, both having talked non-stop during our late-afternoon sandwiches.

"It doesn't look good John- I couldn't get anything that he couldn't explain away. He's got a decent excuse for why he didn't want to play ball with you initially. He couldn't get his friend to give him the receipts. You put him between a rock and hard place and he needed time to try and get receipts for all the under-the-table work the guy did to rebuild the boat. Your guy didn't do anything wrong, he was just trying to save a buck."

"Yeah but it's real convenient how the boat builder is a ghost now and there is nobody else that saw the boat in the water."

"True, but that's not his problem, that's yours. He shows enough cash outlays to cover the labor and materials for the rebuild. I bought us a little time with the other documents, but if he can't produce them, we can't deny him for failure to cooperate. He basically met the requirement. Once he signs off on the EUO and returns the Proof of Loss, you've got a 60 day window to pull the rabbit out of the hat.

"What did you think about his response to the two final questions?" I asked.

"Never saw that before, I have to remember to tell my people to end all their theft EOUs like that. That was beautiful. The guy didn't know whether to wind his watch or soil his pants."

"So I'm onto something," I persisted.

"Yeah but proving it is going to be a bear, you didn't come out of this with anything to really hang your hat on. The guy didn't walk away from this claim, he still thinks he can pull it off."

~

The Insured scrounged the documents up and there was nothing in them to write home about. He and his wife signed their EUOs without any corrections and returned the Proof of Loss. Now that no bombs had dropped on him, he kept up the pressure on us by telling his agent he would follow up on his threats. Time was running out, as I remembered the stern stare from my employer's top alpha male. The boat builder had left no traces. He was into the wind as the saying goes. He owed money to suppliers. He owed his landlord after moving out in the middle of the night. Local marinas wanted to find him too. He had taken healthy deposits on different boats around the area and walked away in the middle of the season with all the jobs uncompleted. It was up to each boat owner to sue him for breaching his contracts. The bad will caused at the marinas was palpable. It looked like he split town and left everybody holding the bag. The marine surveyor did tell me that the builder had bought another boat that was destroyed in Hurricane Bob. Did he buy it for parts? Was he going to rebuild that boat too? The surveyor was checking to see to whom it was registered.

What did I have to work with? The builder was just one person and not a company and he couldn't be found to verify the work and the payments. Nobody had seen the boat after it supposedly rebuilt. Did it even exist? The insured could have taken a picture of another Marlow-Hunter 37 at a mooring anywhere and represented that it was of his boat. That it disappeared before the surveyor could inspect it was huge, especially when we knew that the boat had been a total loss from a hurricane. The hurricane itself was a catastrophe to the boating community in New England and the claims apparatus for this sleepy part of the business was still swamped.

I was swamped with work too. This was only one of my cases. I had a monster case taking up almost all my time in New Jersey involving a staged-accident ring. It made this case pale in comparison. I was running and gunning on multiple assignments throughout the Northeast, grinding out 40,000 miles a year on the company car. I was one busy guy. Finding time to work this case was hard to come by, but since this case had the attention of the hierarchy of my company, it behooved me to shuffle my cases around to finish the job I started.

～

Mattapoisett, Massachusetts is on the way to the Cape. Cape Cod; that is, to the rest of us. Its harbor is nestled in Buzzards Bay. I was hoping to knock on some doors at the last known address of the boat builder and verify the receipts from the materials supplier given to me by Mr. Blowhard at the EUO. I would be shutting the case down if I didn't get anywhere that day. Again, I drove before dawn from Connecticut. I was assured of getting a full day of sunlight to work before driving home.

"Just some bar fights is all, he'd get released when nobody wanted to sign complaints against the other party," The local cop said, "Nice enough guy when he was sober, though."

"Yep, he drives an old blue Ford F-150 pick-up, you'll recognize it when you see it," The landlord said. "He still owes me for two months rent and when you see him, tell him that he can kiss his security deposit good-bye."

"No Ma'am, but thanks anyway," I said to the lonely housewife that lived across the hall from the boat builder's apartment. "A coffee would be nice, but I have a lot of ground to cover today." She hadn't seen him with any women during the time that he lived across the way, both of them on the ground level. She did verify his physical description right down to the mullet and mustache in his mugshots at the PD.

The girl at the local package store hadn't seen her

regular beer customer for a couple of months and was worried that something might have happened to him; same with the diner waitresses and the guys at the pizza joint, where I had a two slices and a coke. I would hit the bars later at happy hour when I had the best chance of catching somebody that might have a line on the guy. There was a neighborhood Blarney Stone on almost every major corner down in this old seafaring town. It would make no difference if it was a weekday or not with his crowd. Any day that ended in the letter Y would be the only requirement for the crowd I was looking for.

"Yeah when his credit was good, we did a nice bit of business with him, but it seemed like he decided to screw us when he owed us the most. Should have seen it coming." The supplier said. He was an older guy; the business had been in his family for three generations. He was taking this dead beat skipping out on him personally.

"Yeah, it was like he decided to stiff everybody at the end; Landlord, boat owners, suppliers. Like he was going to just vanish," I said.

I was looking at the stack of bills. "What's all this stuff mean?"

The old sailing man looked at the bills and said, "Looks like it wasn't going to plan. He was reordering more epoxy and glue than I would imagine he needed."

I showed him the copy of the photographs from when the boat was a total loss up in dry dock. "He turned this into that". He studied the 'after' photo closely. I'd seen fingerprint examiners do the same thing with prints taken from the scene of a crime and compare them with prints from a suspect.

He went back to the bills and shuffled through them again shaking his head. With that much damage on the starboard side. I'd think that he would need a lot of fiberglass to patch up all the holes. He hardly has any."

"Could he have ordered the fiberglass elsewhere?"

"Hold on a sec." He put down the photos and bills and dialed the phone.

Three calls later, he confirmed for me what I was beginning to suspect. This was no ordinary repair. "He didn't get the fiberglass anywhere in Plymouth county. He's got enough glue and epoxy for two boats but not enough fiberglass to fill the holes for even one."

"I know he bought a second boat himself as salvage from the hurricane. Could it be for the other boat?" We were spitballing now.

"Possibly, but that doesn't explain why no fiberglass." the sea-faring man said.

The guy that knew everything about sailboats and the investigator who got sea sick on the Port Jefferson Ferry just looked at each other trying to figure out what was going on. We both knew we were on to something, but that something was eluding us.

Finally he said, "Why don't you go poke around his shop and see what you might find?"

I looked at my notes, "The insured said it was an industrial park in Fair Haven, but he didn't have his driving directions and said that he was there only twice. I was going to canvass the town to try to find it after I left here."

"I can do you one better, young man. We had to deliver a few times to him." He pulled out a receipt that hadn't been given to me by Mr. Blowhard and showed me the delivery address scrawled on the bottom. He then showed me a second one with the same address in Acushnet, the town just North of Mattapoisett. "More glue, both times."

He initialed and dated those two receipts before tearing

off carbonless copies. Both had been billed for delivery to Mr. Mullet and Mustache and not for the insured. I had seen neither copy before today. Why not? Wouldn't they have added to the cost of the repairs? Were these even related to this boat rebuild? Could it have been for another customer or even the salvage piece the re-builder bought for himself? I mulled over this on the way.

His directions were dead on. I pulled into the nondescript collection of single story corrugated buildings set out in no particular order.

I finally found the unit I was looking for. The doors were padlocked, there was no sign on the outside of the building, but the area reeked of glue. I took out my camera and popped a few pictures when a man in a work shirt stenciled with the name *Ned* above the shirt pocket popped up next to me and made me jump almost out of my shoes. He walked over from the machine shop across the alley. You could hear grinding going on from the open bay doors.

"You from the Health Department?" he asked. He was working on several days of a salt and pepper beard and had lifted his safety glasses to his forehead giving him a raccoon look.

"No I am an insurance investigator investigating a boat claim." I handed him my card.

"What kind of boat claim?" Ned asked.

"A guy up by Boston Harbor claims his boat was stolen. Problem is that we never got a chance to inspect it after he put it on the policy. It disappeared before we had a chance to look at it."

"Where'd he lose it?"

"Up near Boston-nobody at the marina had ever seen it there in the water."

"So why are you here?" he asked.

Not knowing if this was a good guy or a bad guy asking me all these questions, I just gave him the honest answer in an aw-shucks sort of way. "The boat had been wrecked in Hurricane Bob and he bought it cheap. The guy that fixed it up for him had his shop there. I said pointing to where I was shooting my camera. "I am just trying to put the puzzle together. The guy that did the repairs is in the wind. I can't find him anywhere."

"Yeah," he said. "A lot of things are in the wind, do you smell the glue?"

I nodded.

"That asshole started gluing the boats together in there and had the fans blowing out here. I thought you were from the Health Department. It was bad. I was getting headaches and even if he didn't huff himself crazy, I thought I was getting high from it. It was really bad. He couldn't keep the door down and he had nowhere else to ventilate the glue when it was setting."

"Whaddyamean, he was gluing the boats together?" I was confused.

"He had two boats and he glued them together and made one boat. Two boats went in there and one came out. I bet he left all his crap in there too."

He saw the expression on my face. I just stood there and was trying picture what he was saying.

"You can't do that with a car," Ned said. "Once a car frame is compromised you can never put it on the road again."

I still wasn't getting it.

Waggling his right hand in front of his chest palm down, Waggling his left hand the same way, he put his right hand on top of his left and stopped waggling them, "He took the boat with a good port side and glued it to the boat with the good starboard side ...... and trashed the damaged sides which are probably still in there."

Now it came rushing at me like a tidal wave Two boats. Two titles. Mr. Blowhard carefully staged it where he showed me the side of the boat that he bought along with the title for that side and poof it disappears. There is still a boat out there with a title that comes from the other boat. "That's why he needed all the glue and none of the fiberglass."

Now it was time for the grinder to look at me. "Huh?"

"I just came from the guy that supplied him with all the glue you smelled. He couldn't understand why your neighbor there needed all the glue but no fiberglass to patch the damage. Now it makes sense. He just slapped the two good sides of the boats together."

~

"Yeah, How'd you know?" The marine surveyor must have thought I was clairvoyant when I told him that the boat the boat-builder salvaged was identical to the boat, Mr. Blowhard salvaged.

"Put it together," I said.

Silence.

"Put them together," I said.

Silence.

"Take the pictures of the two boats and put them together so that both good sides are showing." I could hardly contain my sheer joy at what he was about to see in my mind's spy-glass.

"Holy Mackerel!" Oh my God! That's incredible!" The surveyor was now shouting.

"What's even better," I said. "The insured sat there in his

Examination Under Oath and swore to us about the repair progress. He never said jack-squat about taking the two good halves and sticking them together with epoxy resin and Super Glue. I never would have covered that aspect in a recorded interview. By messing with me, we really made him explain all his movements. He never said anything about the boat builder buying an identical boat and using it to make one."

"Somewhere out there is the boat using the other title with a clean Hull Identification Number."

"The boat builder didn't sell it yet?" I asked.

"Not in Massachusetts at least." He replied. "He's still the registered owner."

We went over scenarios for a few more minutes before he conference called me down to Baltimore. He began jabbering in nautical terms with the Yacht claims manager that first sniffed this one out. The Yacht claims guy was excited about knowing that he was right. Something fishy had been going on.

An hour later, the conference call grew to include my boss and the lawyer and I was getting exasperated.

"His answers were just vague enough about where the repairs were done and what kind of repairs were done," our lawyer said. "You've got to give me more, John."

He was right and I didn't want to admit it. Mr Blowhard was looking smarter than us by the minute.

"Find me the boat," the lawyer said.

"The boat builder won't be far away. We know his truck and his physical description," I said.

The Yacht guys then clued us in that the boat could be anywhere on the East Coast and even possibly in Mexico or the Caribbean. It would be like finding a needle in the haystack. By the time the call ended, the wind was pretty much out of my sails.

~

Time went by slowly until a week before the deadline. We had to deny the claim or pay up. It was that simple. Deny it without rock-solid proof and we ran the risk of seeing a full-page ad in the yachting magazine. Pay and we could still imagine him writing a nasty letter to the editor complaining of his treatment at the hands of the Gestapo. I could only hope that he spelled my name right. My daydreaming was interrupted by a phone call.

"You're buddy's back," he said.

"Who's this?" I replied.

"Ned," he said.

"I'm sorry, do I know you?" I asked.

"You remember looking for the guy that glued the boats together? Well he's back cleaning out his tools. I went over there and asked him what he was going to do about the smell. He said that he was gonna take care of it when he comes back tomorrow."

I now instantly remembered the Grinder whom I had given my card. "What else did he say?"

"Said that he was getting a big payday soon and that he was headed off to Florida in his boat."

"Anything else?"

"Naw, he kept promising me that he would clean it up real nice. Yeah, right, that ain't gonna happen."

"Did you say anything about me?"

"Naw, I figured that you'd want to introduce yourself."

"You figured right Ned. What was he driving?"

"Same ratty pick-up."

"Blue F-150?"

"Yep."

"Thanks Ned, I owe you big time. Do me a favor, don't say anything to him tomorrow."

"I won't be here because I'm going hunting."

"Good. Happy hunting."

"You too, I imagine." Ned hung up.

Things moved quickly then. The next morning two tinted-window vans with long CB antennae followed the boat builder back to the parking lot of a marina in New Bedford without being detected. There, the marine surveyor and I who had been following the chase at a safe distance spotted the boat in the water at a slip with an electric hook-up. The boat builder was living on the boat. On the transom was painted 'Double Trouble'

There it was in plain view. They were mocking us all the time. They were oh- so smart.

The marine surveyor carefully noted the slight differences between the port and starboard sides. Those observations were sworn into a search warrant executed a few days later by the Marine equivalent of the Mass State Police. Also boarding the vessel, when the warrant was executed were the two previous owners of the two boats. They were confused at first, but each noted items that were unique to their remaining portions only they would know.

The man with the mullet and mustache began singing immediately. He said was going to get some traveling money from the claim pay off in one week and he was taking the boat to Florida to make a fresh start. He was walking away from all his debts and only came back to the rental storage unit to get his tools so that he could work on boats in the Sunshine State. He would have been in the wind sooner, if we didn't drag out the claim. He blamed the whole scheme on Mr. Blowhard, who tried to turn the blame around by saying that it was a straight up theft by the boat builder. It was all a big mistake. Blah. Blah. Blah.

In the end, they both pled guilty and the mullet man was socked with the restitution and reimbursement of all our expenses. Mr. Blowhard was going to jail for an attempted theft by deception and fraud. The local papers covered the story, but there was no full page ad in *Boaters World*. Imagine that.

~

Three days after pleadings in open court, Mr Blowhard received a nondescript package in the mail. It was post-marked from somewhere off I-95 along the coast of Maine. Inside was a red box from Old Spice, you would know it instantly by the picture of a sailing ship on the bottle of after-shave. Inside the box however was soap on a rope with a little crayon note nicely written by a six-year-old girl named Emily with two words. *Bon Voyage.*

SHAME

The shrine for Evelyn "Champagne" King was set up in the dining room. Last year, her single "Shame" made the 1977 Top Ten Billboard for an R&B single. Her Platinum Album on the wall hung next to Jesus praying in the garden while his apostles snoozed. Pictures of her with the emerging "Philadelphia Sound" record producers were prominently displayed in frames and on plaques completing the homage. For a West Philly row home, this was a surprise for sure. I was there to interview a family member who witnessed fatal car accident. This was my first job since leaving the PD and I was happy to be out and about in the City of Brotherly Love. As a suburban boy working as a hometown cop, I had become claustrophobic with the prospect of circling the same fourteen square miles on nights, weekends and holidays for the next thirty-two years, before getting the pension at fifty-five.

This was my start as an investigator with a company that provided services for insurance companies nationwide and they had me working South and West Philly. I'd drive downtown before rush-hour to their offices in Center City overlooking Independence Hall to bang out my triplicate reports on an electric typewriter and make appointment calls on a black dial phone that I shared with Cornell. (He made a point to wipe off the receiver every time with his handkerchief before he would touch it to his ear.) Mid-morning, I'd retrieve my '72 canary yellow Toyota Corolla and hit the road. I tried to make my stops as efficient as possible working leads down through the Italian Market into the South Philly neighborhoods to Tenth and Oregon and savor a hoagie or cheesesteak at my favorite stand-up in the shadows of Veterans Stadium where my beloved Phillies and Eagles played and occasionally won. I'd read Dolson in the Inquirer or Quinn and Conlin in the Daily News to get my Sports Page fix, then head out to stops past the Airport and the swamps. It was rumored the Mob dumped the stiffs that crossed them there in the marshy fetid muck, never to be heard from again. I'd continue on through Southwest into West Philly, then jump on the Schuylkill Expressway for a half-hour ride to the brick-twin that my new bride and I called home in Bridgeport, PA.

It was the middle of a heat wave, on a sweltering August day with no AC in my stick-shift. I was tugging on the company-mandated tie to loosen it while coaxing any breeze into the windows of my econo-box. My eight track tape player, mounted below the dash, kept me humming to Todd Rundgren, an Upper Darby boy done good, as I rolled down her street.

Older and walking with an unsteady gate, the lady of the house greeted me after I rang the bell. She would be with me shortly I was told, as she was talking long-distance. Mid-day, week-day long-distance phone rates were expensive and certainly increased their importance. After leading me around the dining room table through the shrine, she motioned back to the parlor for me to sit in an overstuffed chair facing her Zenith Color TV. I collapsed into it, realizing how my previous evening's fun and the day's heat had knocked the snot out of me. The evangelist on the tube was really getting worked up about Hell and Damnation. He was red-faced and shaking with righteous rage. I was waiting for him to burst a blood vessel. Contrasting the flame-throwing preacher, the tidy row home was surprisingly cool and pleasantly dark. Heavy drapes kept windows to the southern exposure from frying the interior. On the light stand next to the chair sat her open Bible, reading glasses and a goblet of nuts. I had missed my hoagie stop that day, slamming down a soft-pretzel and a Coke from a cart vendor instead. Sticky hot, nod-off tired and empty-stomach hungry, I fixated on the treats at my elbow. Damn, those nuts looked good. My glimpses confirmed that she was tethered to her phone in the kitchen. She paced past the doorway at long intervals. The longer she talked, the longer I longed for them. Too wrapped up her telephone call to notice me, the lady wouldn't miss a couple, I thought. So I slipped a couple into my mouth and set the goblet down quickly. They were delicious. If God made anything tastier, He kept it in Heaven. A few more wouldn't hurt, I rationalized. Then a few more and then some more.

Before you knew it, the preacher had worked himself into a lather. Mesmerized in my tired stupor, goblet in hand, I suddenly discovered that I had eaten all of them. That's when she walked in staring at the empty goblet and me with a hand-caught-in-the-cookie-jar expression on my face. I started to apologize, but she placed a finger on her lips to shush me.

"That's okay honey, I can't eat them anyway because my teeth aren't good."

Relieved that I hadn't stolen her whole goblet of goodies, I swallowed the last of them and that's when I heard her say ,"I just like to suck the chocolate off them."

Cop Humor. What can I say?

N TEST 8

I trudged out of a quiet probate court in the Connecticut Berkshires into the chilly snow and sleet of late March with my head held low. It seemed that a quirk in the intestacy (when people die without a will, they die intestate) law of the Nutmeg state was exploited by the other side's lawyer and my heir was disallowed. I wasn't looking forward to either the conversation with the heir or with Mrs. Hoda. That case would make a story by itself, but that's for another day.

A few years, earlier, I had a case that introduced me to the high stakes niche of Missing Heir Research. By working that case, I learned forensic genealogy, which is really genealogy on steroids, many times filling out the family tree without the ability to interview the next of kin. I had to locate the estate where a person died without a will and where only some of closest living relatives, but not all, were found. Occasionally, I would run across a case where there were no known living relatives and I would be racing against the estate administrators. In both situations, I would be racing against other missing heir firms to do the research to find the missing heirs. It was exciting, heart-pounding work. I began scanning recent cases in nearby probate courts on Friday afternoons, as a hobby really. Some of the cases had potential and I would work them up only to find out that I was a day or week or month late in contacting them. My competitors had beat me to them. I had to learn from my mistakes or else all that time and energy would be wasted.

Some weeks, I would sift through the files and not get so much as a nugget. It was like prospecting for gold. As I got better and faster at finding heirs, I would find the case and squeeze the research in between my private investigations jobs. When I found living heirs that were entitled to a share of an estate, I would make a cold call door knock. Standing on their door step, I would tell them that when they woke up that morning they didn't know that they were an heir to an estate. I would mention the names in their family tree like I was the distant cousin they never met. If they had not been contacted by my competitors, I could sign with relief. I would offer them a simple one page contract that said I would connect them to the estate about which they had no clue and that I would handle all the expenses for them. The kicker was that I would do so for a percentage of their inheritance. If they said no thanks, they still had 100% of nothing, but if they signed their name on the dotted line, they'd get between 65% and 70% of something. If they balked, I told them to take the contract to a lawyer or somebody they trusted and I told them to investigate me, to contact my references. Some of my references were attorneys that I worked for, some were very happy heirs. My website was optimized to help them see that I was the real deal. Most importantly, I told them that if they got no money, they owed me nothing. It was not easy convincing people, especially older people, that I was legit and the deal was legit without telling them when how or where the family member died.

Just by the mere fact that I showed up on their door step was sometimes enough of a tip-off for them to figure out that old Aunt Matilda hadn't sent them a Christmas card last year. I began piling up some successes and was making some serious side money. This side gig was supplying more income than the PI work and I had to admit that the thrill of the chase was addictive.

The cases took sometimes up to two years to settle and I had laid out money for expenses and in the beginning the lawyers I hired received a percentage of my fee as their fee when the money changed hands. When the bank account started to swell, I hired the lawyers on an hourly basis and expanded my operation into more courts and more days of the week. This well-paying hobby went from part-time to most-time and in summer of 2008, after netting my first six-figure payout and having many more in the pipeline, I went full time with Hoda Genealogy which quickly morphed into International Missing Heir Finders.

I was now late for an appointment with a nearby town's unofficial historian and I slip-slided along Rte. 7 to her house which overlooked the ice-choked Housatonic River. She had to check me out in person before telling me what she had uncovered in vital records. Adoption records for even a card-carrying genealogist like me are not public and she would only tell me verbally whether the subject in one of my cases was adopted or born into the family. This subject's natural sibling's children stood to take or not take in an inheritance depending on this conversation and some real money was at stake. I had to show the historian my driver license, genealogy "Blue Card" and my PI license. Her dogs had to sniff me out too before they settled down in

front of the Franklin stove. This woman was a veritable trea-
sure-trove of town history and I was fascinated by her
painstaking research at all the local cemeteries, churches
and of town records. Her collection was all manuscript, not
in any digital format. She wasn't getting any younger.
Finally, she delivered the bad news that the subject was
adopted by a wealthy family that summered there to escape
the heat of Brooklyn.

I phoned my senior researcher Claire with the bad news.
Claire had done a good job locating this lady and getting us
a lead that led us to closing the case with complete knowledge of kinship. We touched a source of knowledge about
which our competitors camped out in Salt Lake City and
elsewhere did not have a clue. We did it with old-fashioned
shoe leather.

As I drove further South on Route 7 past shuttered
antique stores, Claire told me that she could not get to Westport, CT to look at an odd case that she had found before
they would close for the day. So the choice was mine. I could
get home before rush hour and mope around about my bad
luck or could visit the nice ladies at Westport Probate and
crawl home to a cold dinner after an hour of bumper to
bumper traffic.

People that know me were aware that I would never
drive by a possible lead or a last chance interview. So I kept
slushing past the Merritt Parkway into the trendy town of
Westport. My friends think that the Gold Coast towns of
Long Island and the Connecticut towns of Greenwich and
Westport are where I should always go fishing for files. The
reality is that when one lives in these ultra-rich suburbs, one
is either a lawyer or lives next door to one. Rich people
know how to take care of their money, shelter their income
and make trusts. Their relations scattered around the world

always seem be sending them Christmas cards. Those relations are almost never lost to the estates. These truisms made this case even more odd. The woman had died without a will and her estate was going to her son. But then he died without a will. The nice ladies retrieved both estates for me. He died after Mom and now both estates were being probated with all of her money going to him except for a Medicaid lien. There were ten cousins taking equal slices of his estate. If it wasn't for the eye-popping amount of money involved, I may have passed on this case. Also, there were hints that they were all only paternal cousins and that some maternal cousins may exist. Cousins take equal shares in Connecticut and even one maternal cousin would get a healthy slice. Even better, if one of Mom's brothers or sisters were still alive, this aunt or uncle of the dead son would trump all the cousins and take the entire estate from the Paternal Ten as I soon nick-named them. Oh, the estate was worth a paltry $1,854,000.

Some of my best cases were made late in the afternoon or on a Friday before a holiday weekend and I could sense that this case could be the whale I had been fishing for. I didn't have much time, but I had built up a rapport with these ladies and the nice people in the Town Clerk's office. This death certificate led to the probate file that led to the land record that told me of another estate that rendered a will where the married names and addresses of Mom's sisters were made crystal clear. When the dust settled, two things became clear. First, I had names of all of Mom's siblings that post-deceased her parents and secondly, it was all in public records in the same building as the son's file that had been open for a year without any investigation into the maternal side. That made me wonder. Actually, it raised a rather large red flag.

It wasn't the first time that a vault was closed behind me for the day, as I profusely thanked the clerks for their assistance. But, I had the maternal side started. What was the chance of all of Mom's brothers and sisters not having children? It had happened to me before where I tracked down the obituaries of nine siblings and none of them had children. Talk about rolling snake-eyes or pulling the handle and getting lemons.

I crawled home jabbering to Claire and reading off names, dates of death, maiden names, married names and addresses. The family tree was forming in my mind and on her desktop. With the power of the internet, Ancestry.com, FamilySearch.com, ObitsArchive.com, the Connecticut Death Index, the 1910, 1920 and 1930 Federal censuses and Westport/Norwalk City Directories, this family tree bloomed.

In quick time, Claire trekked to the State Library where it seems that every CT newspaper ever printed and the New York Times is on microfilm. Microfilms of obituaries now delivered us with the names of maternal cousins. More internet research followed by a brisk walk three blocks to the State's Office of Vital Statistics began filling out our certified documentation of the maternal side of the family: who was living, who was dead, married names and out of state towns where they lived. This was a heady time. The thrill of finding this side of the family was only tempered by the what-ifs. What if they were already found by the estate and for some reason those records were not in the permanent file? What if my competitors found this file a year earlier using my same methodology? What if I can't find them? What if I can't sign any of them to my contract?

My Licensed Professional Investigator skills kicked in and I found five maternal cousins immediately, and then the break-neck speed of the Find turned into the Siege of Leningrad in the Sign-up phase. So instead of the Paternal Ten keeping the whole pie, one-third had to be sliced off for the maternal side and one-third of that third going to me, if I signed them all. If it all worked out I'd net about $180,000 after paying my lawyers. More than I ever netted in any of the previous years of full-time PI work.

Luckily, they had not been contacted by the competition. With so much money at stake, I had to be careful not to tip my hand. I had to do one sign up at a time and could not mention where the estate was or how much money was involved. They were determined to find out where the estate was located and cut me out of my fee. One heir could only call from a pay phone away from her house, because her husband was convinced this was a scam. I was confounded by a hard-headed heir that would not sign my agreement under any circumstances. His siblings could not prevail on him, he wouldn't listen to reason. A month dragged by. I only had three of five heirs signed up to my contingency-fee contract. I had their numbers on speed dial. One heir was off the radar-scope, but with threads of information gleaned from these interviews and our research, I found him living in a group home and he was under guardianship. His lawyer never returned my calls and seemed happy to drive me nuts by wanting to negotiate my fee, learn the location of the estate before signing my fee, getting approval of the court where his client was conserved, consult the tide tables and generally make me bleed through my eyeballs.

The difference between signing heirs to twenty per cent of the estate and one-third was a number followed by five zeros. This difference was more money than I had earned for my entire first year as a PI and it was hanging in the balance. Finally, I told Claire that we had to look at the paternal side of the family to see if they kind of, sort of, forgot any other cousins on their own side. 4/16th was nicer than 3/15th by 5 % and could take some of the sting out of not signing the hard head and the special needs heir.

Claire picks up the story here with plucky Brit understatement.

"With two maternal heirs refusing to sign, the size of our slice was in jeopardy and John was eager for me to go back to the paternal side and attempt to uncover some black sheep cousins. Armed with my list of deceased paternal aunts and uncles, I headed to the State Archives newspaper room and began retrieving microfilm. I had found four of the five obituaries and although there was the possibility of an additional cousin, he didn't share the family name and things didn't look promising. I had one more obituary to obtain and fed it into the machine. A man came up to me and asked if I had almost finished and I said I would just be a couple of minutes. However, this obituary was much older than the others and the front page of that newspaper lacked an index so I began the painstaking task of going through each page looking for the right section. After a few minutes of unsuccessful searching, I reluctantly gave up my machine and vowed I would return at a later point to find that elusive obituary. The next week I went back and tried again and this time I found it. Well, at least I thought it was the right one. As I read through the list of survivors, several of the names matched what I already knew but there were five names that I had never heard of before, supposedly the deceased's father's siblings. I read through the obituary several times as I tried to wrap my head around what it was telling me, that I found five additional aunts and uncles. If any were alive that changed everything.

I hurried back from the newspaper room and started up

my computer. I needed to find out who was alive and who was not. My heart was pounding as my fingers flew on the keyboard, typing the different names into the Social Security Death Index. After about thirty minutes, I had determined that at least two of the five were deceased, one had died in 1991 and the other in 2005. I grabbed the relevant microfilms and found their obituaries. As of 2005, the three that had previously been unaccounted for, were still alive. I ran their names in our people finder database and obtained their contact details. It was only then that it fully dawned on me as to what I had uncovered."

A few minutes later, Claire called me again and asked me if I was sitting down. I told her that I was driving and she cautioned me to pull over. She then stunned me speechless. The son's paternal grandfather had fathered a second younger family and there were two living half-aunts and a living half-uncle of his. Connecticut intestacy law treats half bloods as whole bloods and aunts/uncles trump cousins; they closed the door to the candy store behind them leaving the cousins out on the sidewalk drooling. That meant that now those three heirs stood to take the entire estate and if I signed them up for one-third and with attorney's fees removed, I would net just under $600,000. This was by far the most money ever in play at this stage of the process for my fledgling company.

Two of these elderly heirs had health issues and money was not growing on trees for them. Their adult children and a grandchild helped them sign my agreements. I visited with the third heir and her son and daughter in-law on a nice spring day. We sipped lemonade in the shade, while I regaled them with one story after the next. She signed and I had contracts on all three.

After the Russian winter with the maternal cousins, this

was like a spring-time walk in the park. Things were looking up, but we still had some big hurdles in front of us. We still had to prove this case and some documentation was eluding us. We also needed to have some big guns represent us in court, otherwise this case could drag out for years with the lawyers bleeding the estate and my pockets.

I had found the gold mine, but not the money to pay lawyers to help me stake a legal claim to it. For the first time in owning my own PI business, I had to think about taking out a loan. Other than paying off a couple zero percent credits cards, I had never approached my wife about putting a mortgage on our house that we worked so hard to pay off. I had to re-mortgage my house to finance this litigation and there was no guarantee of success or a speedy result.

She is much more risk-adverse than I am and now I was asking her to help me in my business and possibly have to begin making mortgage payments again. It wasn't an easy discussion. I called it a gold mine. She called it "invisible money". Neither of us had a magic ball. I had to run it by two very good lawyers and when we talked, I didn't wax poetic. My usual verbosity was truncated by the vision of a taxi-cab meter whirling out of control. They could not guarantee a speedy result, nor one that was 100% iron clad.

My wife and I went over the family finances, our expenses and what the mortgage would do to us if the case didn't pan out. Finally, it was decided that if the case didn't pay off, I would pay the balance of the loan off from my 401K and there would be an early withdrawal penalty. I was ready to spin the wheel on this case. I didn't know the odds of this high-stakes game, but I knew what it would cost if I lost.

I hired the lawyers and the time finally came to tell the heirs where the estate was located, who died and how much money was involved. The lawyers, Claire and I had the heirs and their adult helpers all connected for the conference call. No matter how difficult my work is sometimes, there is nothing harder that breaking the news of death to a family member. The Publishers Clearinghouse Sweepstakes euphoria has to be tempered with a discussion about the Grim Reaper. You never know how it is going to play. I knew these people by now and they trusted me. I had to be super sensitive to their needs now at the time of disclosure. When I turned my cards over, there was silence, as they processed this information. They slowly talked about their memories of the son. It was clear that this second family was connected to him. It was also becoming clear that some of The Paternal Ten knew of their half-aunts and half-uncle. One claiming cousin was still writing regularly about family matters with one of the half-aunts. My heirs knew some of the maternal cousins and found it strange that the paternal cousins didn't know about the maternal cousins. I expected more anger from them, but I learned from them that after this was all over, they would have to pick up the pieces with The Paternal Ten and still be a family. That level-headed thinking blew me away. It also helped their posture in the free-for-all that was about to begin.

Just before Memorial Day in 2009, we dropped the bomb on the court on the same day we sent a copy of our research and contracts to The Paternal Ten's counsel. You could hear birdies tweet and pin drops for the next couple of weeks. The court was stunned and The Paternal Ten didn't know what to say.

We received a court date and on the day we arrived at court some of the Ten were there. One looked at me and said, "that's the guy who stole our money".

In the court, the kindly judge realized that this matter

could get ugly and allowed some chatter, but made it known
that he was in charge. The other side filed a motion without
giving us our courtesy copy until we arrived. Claire and I
read their rebuttal to our research with heart's pounding.
When we finished, I thought about my fourth grade
teacher's red pen on my grammar and punctuation. They
were shooting at an aircraft carrier with peashooter. There
is a saying amongst lawyers that when you don't have the
law, you pound on the facts and when you don't have the
facts, you pound on the law, and when you don't have either,
you just pound on the table. They did a lot of pounding on
the table that day and our lawyers remained calm. Round
one ended with us having to respond to the motion, but
another date was set in short order.

We responded with even more proof. Our heirs
produced affidavits, photographs and other memorabilia of
their father and how he was a part of both families' lives.
The next couple of hearings were a blur with discussions ad
nauseam about DNA, paternity and illegitimacy. The law
was clear about half and whole blood and aunts/uncles
taking to the exclusion of cousins. One of The Paternal Ten
hired a divorce lawyer who made noises and even the
maternal cousin's conservator showed up (a good billing
day). The tactics reminded me of how during the endgame
of the Korean war, the Chinese were arguing about the
height of the chairs and the dimensions of the actual peace
table each day while sending suicide charges against the
GIs. They wanted to wear the Allies down to get a better
outcome when the carnage stopped. Just like the Allies, we
stood firm and never yielded.

By the fall, my resources were getting thin. The amount
of the second mortgage was exhausted. Neither lawyers had
ever seen such obstructionist tactics in a probate case

before. I was now meeting payroll from cash advances on my credit card. Finally, I had to ask the lawyers if I could delay my next payment and future payments until after the estate distributed.

It finally boiled down to the other side making the argument that since we could not produce a marriage certificate of the son's grandfather's marriage to the mother of my heirs that they were illegitimate.

Again Claire tells the story of her research. "In preparing the documentation for the court so that our new heirs could take, it was clear that the son's grandfather had left a pretty substantial paper trail. Firstly and most surprisingly, he appears in the 1930 census twice! Then in his World War One draft registration his person of contact is his first wife and in his World War Two draft registration it is his second wife. The other side tried to argue that this was not the same person, but with the same first, middle and last name and the same birth date, that argument just seemed ridiculous. In talking with the heirs, we learned that the first wife died in 1933 and the decedent's grandfather moved in with the second woman, taking his young children from the first marriage with him. This merging of the families can be seen in city directories. Despite our overwhelming evidence, the court wanted a marriage certificate, the one document we had not been able to retrieve. A marriage date was hinted at in the second woman's probate, but if that was right then we had a bigamy situation on our hands. Unable to find any trace of a marriage in Connecticut, we crossed over the border and contacted a genealogist in New York."

Waiting for this one piece of information went from days to weeks and then months. The bureaucracy of New York State government plodded along. I began cashing in Savings Bonds that my parents gave me when I was a kid. Finally, when it looked like we were stymied, we received a call from our Albany genealogist who obtained the genealogy copy of the marriage certificate. The court told us that it had to be certified. Knowing the town now where they got hitched, I was camped out on the town hall door step when the town clerk opened the doors the next morning. The next day, the certified copy was in the court's hands and we had checkmated the Paternal Ten. On December 3rd, the court determined our heirs to be the rightful heirs to the estate. We celebrated. We asked for a partial distribution and the other side agreed. They were tired of spending good money and wanted to lick their wounds. We waited and waited. My resources were nearly exhausted.

On the morning of Christmas Eve day 2009, I had paid bills and had a balance of $47.36 in my checking account. All my overdraft accounts and credit cards were completely maxed. After New Years, I would have to tap my IRA just to pay for groceries. These past months were hard on my wife. She trusted me, but had a hard time understanding why all this legal maneuvering was taking so long. It had taken a toll on our usual Holiday cheer.

What started out as side gig making me some nice Cha-Ching while I ground out respectable billable hours as PI a few years earlier, now, with this one rainmaker case, was about to wipe out my retirement accounts. I began to realize that the other parties around the roulette table could keep taking spins until the dealer told them to stop. Could they file an appeal and place the money in a holding account while the appeal was heard? Were they trying to wear me down for a settlement?

Before lunch I was ready to close the books on the business for the year and it was abysmal. The red ink and the outstanding loan balances guaranteed that I'd be working for the rest of my life. Visions of that old bent-over guy pushing carts in the supermarket parking lot, and not sugar plum fairies, danced through my head.

We got dressed for the late afternoon's children's church service where we attended and talked about how excited the kids were for Christmas and the gifts we had gotten them. After the service, we would go to our favorite Indian Restaurant, one of the few eateries open on the night before Christmas.

Out of habit mostly, I checked email one last time before getting the car ready for our trip to church. I don't know what I was expecting. Good news and glad tidings had been hard to come by lately.

It was 3:10 PM and I had to read it twice to make sure my lawyer was not being naughty, but nice. I sat down in the car and read it out loud to my family. My lead lawyer emailed to inform me that $1,000,000 was wired into his account that morning. Santa came early and was very nice to John and his heirs.

I called the lawyer and put him on the car's speakerphone. I thanked him profusely, but not before asking why he sat on the good news until the end of the day. He told me that he was duty bound to tell the heirs first and didn't get a return call until just before he emailed me. I was very happy that he shared the good news with them. What a Christmas present for us all!

On December 29th, my company received our first check on the case for $321,308.13. Red ink turned to Black and what I thought was going to be a catastrophe turned out to be my best year ever. I know the exact amount because a copy of it is framed on my office wall along with the second marriage certificate and the obituary that alerted us to the second family. The estate continued to pay out and the last of the big payments made for happy times.

Here's the kicker; had the Paternal Ten shared the pie with the Maternal Five and supplied the court with a nice big family tree showing all the cousins, I would have seen a large extended family sharing equally. Instead, they got nothing. I paid off all the debts, gifted my wife the dream kitchen she always wanted and have a great story to tell to go along with the candy apple red sports convertible in my garage with a license plate that reads

N TEST 8.

TRICK OR TREAT

"Can you describe them to me, ma'am?" It was the one night of the year when you could be guaranteed getting a good description out of an eye-witness.

"Well, one of them had a hatchet and blood coming out of the bandages wrapped around his head and another was Little Red Riding Hood. There was a Nurse and Dracula too," she continued, "yeah and there was the cowboy, a baseball player, and the kid with an oversized coat buttoned up to look like he had no head. I don't know them from the neighborhood. I only turned my back for a second and they took it all. I don't have anything left for the other kids." These marauding candy stealers arrived on foot, a roving gang of ne'er-do-wells.

I had to chuckle at the call on this warm Halloween night and at my good fortune, as I cruised around the upscale Blue Bell, PA neighborhood. For this, the Bicentennial year, my Chief had convinced the town fathers tourists from all over the world would swarm Philadelphia and its suburbs like locusts. My hiring was the answer to the road-clogging hordes that never materialized. I was a twenty-one year old rookie working in my hometown on the 3-11 shift.

It wasn't long before I spotted them. In my deepest Marlboro man voice, I said, "hold it right there mi amigos." I wasn't letting seven years of Spanish in high school and college go to waste.

I got out of the Black and White and adjusted my Second Chance bullet proof vest. I made a show of placing my nightstick in its ring on my Sam Browne belt. Loved making that move, just like on Police Story or Adam-12.

"I can throw you all in the back of my squad car and haul you to the Police Station and make your parents pick you up or you can march back to that nice lady's house and give her back her candy." I could out-stare any bunch of ten year old kids from the burbs. Philly may have been a different matter.

I drove back to her driveway as the band of now not so merry men made their way back into her house.

I was about to make them give her all of their candy until she said, "they did the same thing to my neighbor across the street. She just came over and told me."

"Okay you guys, we're going across the street to give back the rest of the candy."

I led the rag-tag bunch of petty thieves across the lawns. The full moon's light bounced off their plastic masks. We made our way up her steps, rang the bell and waited. I thought about the cooling dew on my polished black shoes and remembered how it soaked my sneakers when I went door to door trick or treating. My best memories were on mischief night though, always the night before Halloween. My parents, in their wisdom, turned a deft ear to my plaintive cries and didn't dare let me go outside, knowing the kind of mayhem I would have created. Instead, I sat in the attic over our doorway entrance, a sentinel keeping a keen eye for the dastardly door-bell ringers and wily window soapers. Of course, I had a big pot of ice cold water ready to dump on the unsuspecting trespassers. Only had to use it once, nine years earlier when I was in seventh grade. Word got out fast to leave the Hoda hacienda on Daws Road alone.

My reverie was interrupted when the other victim opened the front door with a whoosh. She looked through the screen door first at me, then at the kids in their get-ups and bags of loot, then back at me. She shouted over her shoulder to her hubbie in the downstairs den. He had the TV turned up too high. "Harry. HARRY! You have to come here to look at this." She was staring right at me with a big grin. "This is the best costume ever!"

359 PETERBILT

"She murdered him for the insurance money and then ran off with her boy-toy to Hawaii."

"And how do you know that?" I asked.

"The owner of the trucking company we insure has been hearing gossip from his other truckers, who are catching bits and pieces from around their small town and the truck stops."

"Town, what town?" I wasn't convinced that this was a claim I wanted to take on.

"Houlton, Maine."

"Where's that?"

He pulled out his atlas from under his desk and looked it up. He stabbed his finger on almost Canada.

I banged my coffee mug down on his credenza. "Christ, can I go any farther?" For almost two years, I had been putting 40,000 miles a year on my company car and that was a God-awful amount of windshield time. They had me running from New York City and North Jersey to all over New England.

"At least it's not winter time," the workers compensation adjuster said.

I nodded. This company and the previous company I worked for had a knack of assigning suspicious claims to me in Maine during the frozen tundra months. Mainers would joke about ten months of snow and the two months of rough sledding during which time mosquitoes replaced the moose as the state animal.

Over dinner that night, I explained to my wife and kids why Daddy had to go away for a couple overnights again. "The last time they saw the truck driver alive was at the American Eagle Truck Stop in Southington, Connecticut. He'd been missing for a couple days when his employer got an anonymous call from Pottle's truck stop in Bangor. 'Your driver's handy by the Boston Morgue.' is all the caller said before hanging up. That's when they identified his body. He'd been shot with a small caliber bullet in the head and dumped two feet away from Boston Harbor. The truck is nowhere to be found."

"So what does that have to do with insurance?" my sharp as a tack ten year old son asked.

"When he was at the truck stop, he was on a run for the trucking company and was coming back from New York City. He was working. His wife is claiming that he died during the course and scope of his employment."

"So why are they questioning it then?" my wife asked. "What was in the truck worth stealing?" Living with me was an education in policy coverages and exclusions.

"That's the strange part, Hon, he was coming home empty. Dead-heading is the truckers' slang for it. Did they kill him just to steal the truck? We don't know. There was plenty of opportunity to steal it while he was inside the truck-stop eating dinner and taking a shower."

"Yeah, but he would know his truck was stolen and report it right away and they wouldn't get very far," my son said.

Smart kid.

"So let's say his wife did kill him for the life insurance, she would not be entitled to any Workers Comp money because his death had nothing to do with his work. He was killed for another reason," I said.

"Why would she do that?" my four year old daughter piped up. For the longest time, she thought I was a frog investigator; that I carried a large magnifying glass and examined green and yellow frogs. We all realized then this conversation was really PG-17 and not for her ears. Since she was born, my talk about insurance fraud had never been about people getting killed. I was about to investigate a homicide. Mommies killing daddies was still a foreign concept to her. Thank God.

∾

Bonnie Raitt's latest album, Luck of the Draw, played on my Dodge Dynasty's cassette player. Three years earlier, she won four Grammys with her comeback album, Nick of Time. I had been a big fan till she all but disappeared after Warner dropped her from their label. Bonnie and I were taking a gorgeous drive through a spectacular leaf-peeping season of New England. This was a perk of being a road warrior. Every fall, I looked forward to the changing colors. It could take the sting out of 14 hours on I-95 to the Canadian border. I would get in late and tired, but I had the entire back list of her works on cassette and the exploding reds, yellows and oranges this Fall of 1992 to keep me company.

"He was like a son to me," the insured said, "I want to know who did this and why." This man was a big man physically and a big man around Aroostook county, or "The County" as the largest county East of the Mississippi was called. His trucking company would haul potatoes or lumber down into the densely populated Northeast and then bring back all kinds of goods as a transfer agent to the Canadian border when he could arrange a pick-up at customs. "His 359 Peterbilt was special and he took immaculate care of it. This was a throwback to the days of the long-nosed Peterbilts with the oval headlights." He slid a picture of the now dead employee standing along side of the cab. The lanky guy with the bushy blond hair grinned in front of his prized possession. "This was the Cadillac of Sleeper Cab Diesels. Maintained right, he could get a couple of million miles out of her."

"It looks like a collector's item, shouldn't be too hard to spot. That cuts both ways," I said as I began to understand why this was more than just another claim to the man.

He agreed, "It's definitely a prize, but you can't drive it on the interstates. Find the truck and you'll find the killer."

My company agreed. "I am authorized to tell you that we agree to match your $25,000 reward for the arrest and conviction of the person or persons responsible. Once your drivers started chatting it up on the CBs and posting this picture on every truck stop bulletin board, we should get a hit."

"$50,000 will loosen up a couple tongues," he said.

∿

As the busboy stacked our plates, we both sat staring silently into our coffee mugs.

Finally, the retired cop-fledgling private investigator finished his thought. "And he never came back to tell me what was on his mind."

The diner was like any small town diner where everybody knows everybody and he picked the place for good reason. It probably made the best pancakes in The County to go along with the bottomless cup of coffee. I found it from my motel easily enough, after I scraped the layer of frost from my windshield that chilly morning after my meeting with the Insured. The Insured urged me that I should meet the PI and hear what he had to say. I now learned that there was much more to this claim than I could imagine.

"He had come to Jesus, just before his last trip and wanted to confide in me." The PI knew all the players here and more. "The driver wasn't always coming home empty, I suspect," he said.

The former cop's prior contacts in the Organized Crime units said that a well known motorcycle gang with affiliates all over the country was rumored to be in charge of smuggling, fencing stolen goods, and moving cigarettes from the southern low tax states to Canada, along with the usual gun and drug running. It was a sophisticated operation. Then there was the not so discreet situation where the grieving widow was on a long vacation in Hawaii with her boyfriend, betting on the life insurance proceeds and the workers comp benefits to pay out any day.

"The driver was set up at the American Eagle Truck stop for a reason. The wife grew up a few towns over interstate I-691 and it was the long-time home of one of the gang's affill-ates. A phone call or two and the shooter would know exactly when the driver would be there," he continued.

Loose threads were becoming connections of how the Special Investigations Unit could delay payment. I never had an insurance case like this and knew that I might not ever catch a real-life homicide again. Sitting there swirling cream into my mug, the story also swirled around my head. The truck driver could have been running contraband in an international smuggling operation run by a North American motorcycle gang and a contract hit was ordered to shut him up before he could cleanse his soul in confession to the PI.

The second scenario that seemed to be the working hypothesis was that the driver's wife wanted him dead, while on the job, so she could collect a double payout.

Both scenarios were possible. Catching a bullet from a would-be truck thief was the least plausible third scenario.

The body was dropped in Massachusetts a few feet from the Boston Harbor instead of with the fishes where he would possibly never be found. Why Massachusetts and not Connecticut? Why put the body on display and why there? The truck was still missing so it could look like a truck theft gone bad. Connecticut was the last place he was seen alive. You had jurisdictions in two different states looking into the death, never a good recipe for success, but at least the Feds weren't big-footing the case. There were people to interview throughout New England and New York.

How could I justify the time to devote to this one case? I had a very active case load of cases worth much more money. I sized up the PI and realized that he could handle all the Houlton leads, we could meet with the two Law Enforcement Organizations (LEOs) and he could liaise with them, talking cop to cop with them, and I could run the leads in CT and the dead guy's last stop before the truck stop - the Hunt's market in the Bronx.

≈

The driver had given a ride to "The Cat Lady". She travelled the east coast and was a frequenter of the truck stops. She was the person who told Security at the American Eagle that the truck left with some of her belongings in the truck. Her complaint also coincided with information as to when the truck was waved through security. No, the guard didn't remember the driver, No, there was no security camera footage. Yes, there was a gas slip and shower ticket signed by the driver. No, there was no way of knowing if whoever stole the truck did it there or after the truck left the truck stop. I asked the Insured's other drivers to put the word out that I needed to talk to her. I knew her real name and her family. I had her previous addresses, but ran into a brick wall.

Ditto with the receiving supervisors at Hunt's market. They produced their copy of the bill of lading and shipping manifest, but no real leads. I even asked for the trucks that may have been loading or unloading at the same time as the driver and those leads didn't pan out. The LEOs were always polite, but were masters in the give and take game, all take and very little give.

It was a cold afternoon in early spring of the following year, when I made my way up the driveway to the front door of the driver's brother in-law's house, a short hop from the truck stop. The PI had learned that the driver and his brother in-law were to meet for dinner while the driver was in Connecticut on that fateful day. It was also developed that the wife, soon to be widow, was in southern coastal Maine in a well-to-do resort town at the same time that her brother and husband were to meet. Since Maine is larger than the rest of New England combined, her presence three hours away from her brother in central Connecticut and one hour from the dump site was found to be very coincidental.

She had since lawyered up when she learned that she

was the focus of the investigation. But there she was in the driveway. The LEOs told me that she was a knock-out and when they interviewed her, she was wearing very skimpy clothing and paraded about for them to ogle her. Today was no different when she met me on the driveway. Standing outside, barefoot with just a negligee on, I worked hard to maintain eye contact with her, I really did.

I asked, "Is your brother home? I have to talk to him about the murder and the missing truck."

No introductions were needed. I knew who she was and she knew that I was just another suit trying to figure out how she did it.

"Nope, He's not here. He's at work," she said.

"Would that be the home heating oil place over on South Colony Road?" I asked.

Most women would cross their arms over their chest, not her. She looked me straight in the eyes, daring me to lower my gaze.

"You could try there," she said. She didn't act surprised that I knew where he lived and where he worked. This was one cool customer.

"But on a day like today he's probably out making deliveries," she said.

I reached into my coat pocket and then extended my hand out to her.

"Here's my card, please have him call me when you see him."

She reached out and slowly ran her fingers across my knuckles and thumb before tugging on the card. She looked back into my eyes and smiled slightly. Then she turned around first to allow me the view, as she slowly jiggled her way back into the house.

As I closed the door to my car and started it, I turned my

headlights on. I recalled how her headlights were turned on. With my breath fogging the inside of the windshield, I muttered, "that was wild." Had I just met a murderer? Did she set her husband up for the MC gang to hit him? One thing she wasn't.; she wasn't an innocent player in the killing.

As the weather got warmer, the trail got colder and the pressure to settle the case was mounting. The Special Investigations Unit can argue, cajole, plead for more time to investigate a case, but there are other factors such as lawyers' fees, bad faith actions, and adverse publicity that factor into the decision. I was no closer to proving the wife had ordered the hit or that the MC Gang did it to silence the driver forever. Then a call from the countryside West of Boston came in to me. The caller said he knew where the truck was located and asked if the reward was still valid.

I finally had a chip to play in the poker game with the LEOs. I told the caller that payment would be made, if finding the truck eventually led to the arrest and conviction of the thief. We haggled a bit and I didn't act all that interested in giving him the money, which he probably took as that this was just another case for me. We agreed to meeting near the recovery site and he would lead me to it.

The LEOs howled that they wanted to talk with the source. I told them that I would meet the source and he would take me to the scene and I would call them. They were not cutting me out of the loop. We finally agreed that they would follow me at a distance.

So at the appointed time, date, and place, I met the source in a public place. From there it was a strange caravan, but it worked, as the source took me over country roads to a truck repair shop with plenty of outside parking.

There she was, parked in plain view once you were well

into the property, but not noticeable from nearby roads. The distinctive elongated nose and the oval "throw back" head-lights were just like the picture I was provided. I sensed that she held the clues that we all were searching for. I had been looking at every Peterbilt that crossed my path for months and here she sat.

Little did I know that by the time CSI was done and the LEOs chatted with the repair shop owner, they had the murder scene in their hands and a name and address of a trucker that was "storing it " there. Some of the cat lady's stuff was still in the sleeper compartment. Things moved very quickly then. The trucker's girlfriend cooperated with the LEOs and enticed her boyfriend back from Texas where he was long-hauling for a company there and they appre-hended him at Logan Airport.

He confessed to being an MC gang wanna be and was told that part of his initiation would be to steal a truck. Little did he know that when his accomplices drove him out to the truck, they waited in the truck for the driver to come back to the rig.

At his plea bargain, he put on the record that he was only there to move the truck and that he didn't kill anybody. His undoing, for his participation in the crime, was keeping the truck. He boxed himself into the corner by admitting to being a conspirator to a felony murder.

After his sentencing for 40 years, he agreed to talk with me and the PI. It was my first time walking into a prison to conduct an interview. The corrections officers studied our credentials and they scrutinized our driver's licenses, even though an appointment was granted in writing. The heavy metal doors closed behind us before similar doors opened in front us, but not until the CO felt like opening it. Behind tinted windows and unseen to us, they were playing the control freaks. Finally, it opened and we were directed by a guard to a cramped windowless room with a bolted down table and three plastic chairs. Again, the waiting game continued. The PI and I compared notes one more time on what we wanted to cover. We both knew this case like the back of our hands and had run hypothetical scenarios over and over again, constructing and deconstructing them with each new fact learned.

Both of us had been schooled in reading body language and knew the kind of questions to ask to elicit responses of both verbal and non-verbal reactions. These questions were disruptive and wouldn't allow the subject to stick to a rehearsed script. My training in Scientific Content Analysis would allow me to read the transcription of the interview later to look for signs of deception.

Finally, a door opened from the end of a long hall and the trucker turned thief and now convicted accomplice to murder shuffled down the hall. He was an imposing figure until he sat down across from us.

We established rapport with small talk and introduced the tape recorder and a three pack of 90 minute mini-cassettes. The PI took notes while I handled the questions. We were in no rush to get to the good stuff. He was a big kid really and the reality of 40 years in jail was now setting in for him. He was happy to talk about his life before getting seduced by the allure of riding with a motorcycle gang. We were introduced to his cadence, speaking voice, his manner-isms and ticks. He didn't want to admit to some of his actions during his initiation, but was clear about what he was asked to do. He was told that he was to steal a truck with very expensive cargo in the trailer and for his efforts he was told he could keep the truck. On the night in question, they drove out in nervous silence. He was then told to wait until he saw the headlights flash and he would know that his accomplices had successfully hot-wired the truck for him to drive off the lot. Neither the PI nor I were prepared for what we heard next.

"I climbed into the cab and smelled gun powder. Right away, I could tell something went wrong. I looked into the sleeper cab and saw a guy laying there motionless. There was blood on the floor of the cab. I asked them what happened. *The wannabe* looked like he was going to get sick. *The shooter* said that the dead guy had come back to the truck and surprised them while they were trying to hot-wire it. Funny thing was, I didn't see anything wrong with the ignition and all I had to do was start the truck with the key that they handed me. It was all wrong, but it was too late for me to back out of it. So I drove the truck out of the truck stop, got on interstate I-84 towards the Mass Pike and Boston with the dead guy right behind me and *the shooter* riding shotgun. When we got close to the Sudbury River, we slowed down and pulled into the breakdown lane and he threw his .22 cal revolver over the railing. We didn't even stop. We were far enough away from the truck stop to ditch the body, but I was told to drive to a specific spot in Chelsea by the water. I was taking orders now about the rest of the plan that I wasn't privy to. The driver was a big guy and we had a hard time getting him out of the cab and onto the ground. I had never been this close to a dead person let alone even handled one before. He was a little older than me and was starting to stiffen up. I figured that we would throw him in the water and make him disappear, but I was told that we had to leave him in that exact spot. From there, we went to a gang member's farm, where we tried to clean out the cab. I was a Zombie. The guy's clothes and his bible were in the sleeper along with a portable TV and some movie video cassettes. There was plenty of junk food. I saw woman's clothes too and dry cat food and kitty litter and a litter box. I was too numb to pay attention to it all. I was told to leave the truck there while they transferred the cargo and come back and get the rig in a couple of days. I got a ride back to the clubhouse. When I left, I knew two things. This was a hit and the trailer was empty. If there was anything in the trailer, it had to be small and light and really tied down. When I was driving, the trailer bounced up and down like a marble on a granite countertop. I've dead-headed plenty of times and know when the trailer is empty. I didn't know then what I know now; that I was set up to take the fall."

He looked like he wanted to cry, but he was already getting hardened by jail.

We went over this portion of his story forward and backwards and in slo-mo. The tape recorder would click every 45 minutes to let us know that we had to turn over the tape or replace it, otherwise we lost track of time.

Did he tell the cops this? Yes, he did. What did they do with the information? Nothing as far as he could tell. The PI and I shot looks to each other while we had him look at photos of the Truck Stop, the 359 Peterbilt and the recovery scene. Our read on this big kid was that he was telling the truth and might have glossed over a few things, but nothing major.

More direct questions and emotion-provoking questions followed. This guy was either a sociopath or telling the truth. Nothing changed in our assessment. We said good-bye to a young man that was staring down the barrel of a 40 year stretch for a murder he didn't commit. The guards played the same game with locking us between the doors, but our muted conversation was far more important than their mind games. Finally, we got outside and breathed deep

the fresh air outside the "super max" prison, a facility designated for gang members and death row inmates. It was the
definition of "hard time".

What we had learned was later verified. The alleged
shooter was a known member of the MC gang with the ties
to the smuggling that the dead driver was about to confess
to before his death. This alleged shooter had beaten a
murder rap previously when the murder weapon, a shotgun, mysteriously disappeared from the Massachusetts
LEO's evidence room. The alleged accomplice was also
known to be a wanna be for the same chapter of the MC
gang as the alleged shooter. None of this mattered to the
LEOs, who were not so buddy-buddy with us now. They
grudgingly told us that both the alleged shooter and alleged
accomplice had solid alibis and no, we couldn't talk to the
alibis ourselves.

The LEOs tied the stolen truck to the thief, who
admitted to being at the scene and told them enough facts
about the murder that they didn't need to prove anybody
else was involved. End of story and end of pleasantries. We
were at odds with the LEOs. The circumstantial evidence
pointed to the motive of silencing the victim from talking,
but it was not enough to move the LEOs in that direction. In
the end, my insurance company had to pay the widow her
benefits. It was a hollow consolation that the insured got his
tractor and trailer back. The source mysteriously stopped
pushing for his reward.

The truck thief went down for the murder and was a
patsy played perfectly by the gang.

Both LEOs cleared their cases, but I was left with a
queasy feeling and tons of unanswered questions. I had a
bulging briefcase of insurance fraud cases that were getting
stale and I had to let this one go.

*Author's note:

Little did I know then, but later in my career, I would see first hand how cases were cleared by arrest, but were not always solved. This was my first homicide case, but not my last. In this writing, I felt the need to tip-toe around some facts, places and names for obvious reasons. I apologize if its recounting was a little stiff.

LUCKY

I was driving in morning rush hour traffic to my Claims Manager job in Norwich, CT on I-95 approaching New Haven. It was a warm dry summer morning. The usual heavy volume of commuters and eighteen-wheelers filled both sides of the highway which was tight here with little room on the shoulders or medians. Not a place to make a mistake or improper lane change. I was clipping along in the far left lane, when I saw what I thought was a black garbage bag against the median. As I got closer, I saw it was a dog and it lifted up its head as I passed. The dog was still alive and was trapped against the median with traffic whizzing by at 65 MPH. I drove by with a sick feeling in my stomach.

This dog was going to die unless somebody did something about it. Who would I call? Whose job was it to handle situations like this anyway? I was dressed in a business suit and was driving my company leased couple year old 1990 Chevy Celebrity, not exactly dressed or equipped for an animal extraction from a busy interstate. I mulled this over as I expertly shifted over three lanes and onto the last exit before the Quinnipiac River. My instincts were taking over before my mind could overrule it.

I committed to moving that dog safely off the highway, before it got mangled. Back on the highway now in the opposite direction. I passed the spot where I thought the dog was laying on the other side of the concrete barrier. At the next exit, I spotted a CONNDOT road crew getting ready to enter the highway to do repairs on the same side of the highway as the pooch.

Perfect. What was the chance of this? They had the right trucks to stop traffic and to safely pull the dog off the State maintained highway.

"You gotta call New Haven's Animal Control," they said.

No matter how I pleaded with or cajoled them, they wouldn't budge. Union rules and not doing another juris-diction's job function was more important than saving a dog's life, I guess. Those #$%^&@!. I just shook my head and got back on the highway.

The traffic going by the dog's position was suicidal to run across, but I observed that traffic going the opposite way was crawling. So I repeated my steps and stopped this time across from the dog's position and ran like a halfback dodging tacklers through three lanes of stop and go traffic and climbed over the waist high concrete barrier to find a scared male German Shepherd looking up at me. The cars were screaming by us at such a speed that I was swaying with each passing car. I was no more than 3 feet away from the double axle trucks. What the hell was I doing out here? The dog was shivering, but seemed to understand that I wasn't there to hurt him. He looked up at me with those pleading eyes and slightly wagged his tail. I didn't see any blood and assessed that I could try to pick him up. Would he bite me or try to get out of my grasp and jump right back into traffic? Would he knock me into the path of a speeding car?

I started waving at the slowing and stopped cars in the opposite lane. I quickly got the attention of a guy in pick-up truck. The sign on the side of his driver's door said he did construction and remodeling.

"Hey, can you give me a hand here. I've got an injured dog over here and we've got to get off the highway. I can sit with it in your truck bed, while you drive".

He looked at me standing on the other side of the barrier in a business suit with rush hour traffic barreling by. Just like me, he had to make a split decision.

Thankfully, he put the truck in park, got out, looked over the median and said, "Hand him to me".

Drivers honking their horns soon saw me bend down and lift the shepherd against my chest. He was hurting, but didn't go for my throat inches away or jump from my arms. I leaned over the barrier and the tradesman took the dog in his chest as I clamored over the barrier to lower his tailgate. I rode with shepherd in the bed of the pick up back to the exit and gave the CONNDOT employees a wave. The middle finger wave.

We found out very quickly where the Veterinarian's office in West Haven was situated. The dog was in pain and protectively curled up again as we bumped and jostled to the Vet's office. The worst was over.

"I think he dislocated his hip, but I won't know if it's broken without X-rays," the Vet said.

"How much?" I asked without hesitation.

"I'll need to take several angles, but I can do it for $150.00," he repled.

This wasn't my dog, but given what we just went through, we were bonding very quickly. I said okay and gave his receptionist my credit card. Maybe, my family would not go to the nice restaurants, I reasoned, for a couple of months, as she ran it though the manual imprinter and handed me a carbon less copy.

The angel of mercy tradesman gave me a ride back to my car and I went on to work with the adrenaline bleeding off.

Later that morning, I learned that the dog's right hip was dislocated and surgery was needed to fix it. All in all, the shepherd was doing better, but he needed the surgery. The Vet had given him a sedative. He suggested the Hamden Animal Hospital.

I called the Hamden Animal Hospital and explained the situation and the surgeon there said he would waive his fee, but it will still cost $250.00. I realized it was a generous offer, but I couldn't take the next step alone.

My wife and I were raising a young family and paying off a steep mortgage on a new house. Where was I going to get that money from? The dog didn't have a collar or tags and neither West Haven, nor New Haven had a report of a missing dog fitting our guy's description. So after much back and forth, my wife agreed for me to pay for the surgery, but she put her foot down about having a full size German Shepherd in the house with our cats. We weren't adopting him.

The next day the surgery took place and was a complete success. My family visited him at the Animal Hospital. His hind quarter was shaved and bandaged and he was still groggy from the anesthesia, but he recognized me and was happy to lick my face. He would soon be well enough to be put up for adoption. My wife loved him, but wouldn't budge.

"Problem is that adult dogs are tough to place. Everybody wants a cute little puppy," the nurse said.

"What happens to adult dogs then?" my wife asked.

"We can keep them for about a month for rehab and then send them to the Animal Shelter. They can only keep them for a short while...." Her voice tailed off.

We all sat in silence petting the dog and realizing that there may not be a rainbow after this storm was over.

Nobody is putting this dog to sleep. Over my dead body. Not on my watch, it's not going to happen, I vowed.

I then remembered I had a friend that was a crime beat reporter at the New Haven Register. The paper occasionally ran stories about hard to adopt pets next to the obituaries.

"I can call the New Haven Register, I think I can sweet talk them into seeing the human interest story here and convince them to do a piece."

A few days later, I received a phone call from the arts/living reporter. She had heard from my friend how I rescued the dog from the interstate and said that she wanted to give the dog a name to personalize it. It helps increase the chances of adoption, she explained.

"How did Rex or Rocky sound to me?" she asked.

"Lucky," I said.

"That's not a good name," she said.

I replied, "it is, if you're alive after being hit by a speeding car, are seriously hurt and huddled against the median of the busiest highway in Connecticut and some guy comes along at the right moment and another guy with a pick up truck comes along exactly when a pick up truck was needed and the Vet does the X-rays and the Animal Hospital is able to do a successful surgery. I think 'Damned Lucky' is more appropriate, but I'll settle for Lucky."

So a couple days later, Lucky's picture ran along with the article and the Animal Hospital's phones lit up with donations, but no takers.

Just when it seemed like they had to ship Lucky to the

pound, a Coastguardsman said he was mustering out of the service but would be taking a night job. He wanted a good guard dog to be at home with his wife and young daughter for protection. A full-sized German Shepherd would fit that role nicely. He read the article and wanted to meet Lucky. They hit it off immediately. After all, who wouldn't fall for him after what he had been through.

A few days later, we united at the man's apartment. My family met his family and Lucky was healing nicely. He looked happy. He was still very gimpy, but knew what his new purpose was. The man had wanted to meet me and thank me. I wanted to make sure my little guy was in good hands. He was. I was shown a closet full of the donations and get well cards for Lucky.

I had been told that the Surgeon got paid and the animal hospital gave me a full credit on my credit card for the surgery and all the after-care would be paid for by donors as well. The Man opened up his checkbook and asked if I had any out of pocket expenses. He wrote a check to me for the X-rays and I thanked him.

Lucky was home at last.

MY BIGGEST FRAUD CASE EVER

RICO

Labor day weekend was just a few hours away, but I knew from past experience that some of my best cases were made late on a Friday afternoon. I was banging out month-end reports on my trusty Smith Corona typewriter. The carbon-less forms fed into it nicely and my weekend was going to start early. I had brought a coffee warmer upstairs to a spare bedroom that doubled as my home office and took occasional sips of coffee from my favorite mug between reports. I had started a habit of buying ceramic mugs from places around my territory to remind me of the successful cases I had worked.

In another hour, I could get a head start on finishing the painting for our middle bedroom. My wife was full term and we were excited about becoming first time parents. The color was neutral as the baby's gender remained a mystery.

My desk phone rang and it was a claims supervisor from Newtown, Pennsylvania who I just met a couple weeks earlier. I had put on a training seminar at his offices on how to spot red flags in Minor Impact Soft-Tissue (MIST) injury claims.

"We got an odd one here that looks like something you should jump on," he said.

In the two years that I worked for this national insurance fraud investigation arm of the Property and Casualty industry, I had heard that before. Sometimes I chased my tail, but most times, the leads panned out.

He added, " and it involves your favorite lawyer."

After I left the police department in 1978, I took a couple of claims jobs that gave me new skills in policy language and the claims adjustment process. It was during that time period, I kept coming across this same Philadelphia law firm. The claims were cookie-cutter. Three or four people riding in the car, getting rear ended, all treating heavily for hard to diagnose injuries with the same doctors or chiropractors. Whether they sat in the front or in the back or if they were male or female or if that were young or old or thin of heavy, no one broke any bones or bled in any of the accidents. Yet, they all had Lumbar-Sacral sprains and strains that needed exactly 3 months of treatments, X-rays and one orthopedic evaluation by the same doctor. (I nicknamed him Dr. 'Buck and a Quarter' because he charged $125.00 for each evaluation and the findings were carbon-copies of every patient he saw for this law firm.) His report completed the "specials" package. The insurance company representing the striking vehicle owner would have to pay between $3,500 and $5,000 for each injured party in the other car for their pain and suffering or else the case would go to trial in front of a sympathetic jury. Their attorney would get a third of that settlement.

While working for an insurance company and battling this law firm, I learned about my employer. They told me that this law firm was on their radar. The law firm was large volume player in the City of Brotherly Love. I got friendly with the local Special Agents and when an opening came up in 1980, I jumped at the chance to combine my police and insurance skills. It was a lucky year for sure. The Phillies won the World Series and the Eagles went to the Super Bowl. Now two years later, I had this same law firm in my sights.

"Our insured called us in a panic. She was crying hysterically and ranting that she was getting sued and that she was afraid that the lawyers were going to take away her row house in North Philadelphia. That's when she started babbling about how the whole claim was made up at "Big Berthas" kitchen table. How this time she was the hitter and the next time, she'd be a passenger in the car getting hit and she'd make some money. Big Bertha would pay her $300 for this accident. We saw from the Mid-East claim's index that the passengers in the struck car had been passengers in other cars that were rear-ended and made bodily injury claims and a couple had been the drivers of other striking vehicles that hit cars with multiple passengers. Guess who the attorney was in all the claims?" he asked.

"Be still my beating heart. This may be the break we are looking for," I said.

"But here is the odd part. She called us up about 20 minutes later and said that she had made it all up about the accident being fake. She sounded more in control, like she was being coached by somebody else in the room," he said.

"I need to grab your file and get the Postal Inspectors to interview this girl right away, before she completely shuts down," I said.

We made arrangements for him to copy the file and I

would jacket a Self-Initiated case and supply him with a receipt for his file.

Before I gulped the last dregs from my mug and ran out my home to my '80 Ford Fiesta, I was able to catch a Postal Inspector down at their 30th Street offices in Philly . I had met him once before during our company's discussions with Postal about task forcing major fraud rings in the city using their Federal Law Enforcement powers in enforcing the Mail Fraud statutes. Every time somebody licked a stamp and put an envelope in the mail where they were perpetrating a fraud, it was one count. If you were a conspirator to the mail fraud, you could be charged as well. The "specials" packages were mailed in and date stamped by the mail room clerk. The claim forms and statement forms that arrived by mail to support the bogus losses were additional counts. Given the dollar value of the claims, each count was a felony punishable by jail time and fines.

The clock was ticking as I ignored some of the less important traffic laws out to Newtown and did my best Pony Express grab of the file before driving against rush hour traffic on this warm late-summer day.

I made my way into town. Both the 30th Street train station with its majestic columns placed in front of an ornate cavernous interior and the limestone Post Office built during the Great Depression loomed as imposing fortresses guarding the gateway to West Philadelphia and the suburbs. Flashing my credentials to the Postal Police, I came skidding to a stop in front of the main distribution mail center. It made it all seem like I was on a hot call from my lights and sirens days as a cop.

Make way for the insurance fraud response team, a mail fraud in progress call, I thought, as I raced up the stairs, breathless from my pack a day habit and excitement of catching this break. I found my way to the Postal Inspector's offices.

James, the Postal Inspector, to whom I had talked made it clear that he wasn't to be called Jim or Jimmy or Jimbo. I only made that mistake once. His supervisor was waiting for us in the conference room. I explained the phone call and the claim file contents, making sure to point out the date stamps on the mailings to both of them. This was the smoking gun that we were looking for.

It wasn't long before we were on our way to North Philly in James' government issue plain wrapper. It had AC and the FM radio found the classical music button. James was born and raised in South Philly in a predominantly Italian neighborhood. His suit was stylish and he appeared to be fit. My suit was from the discount store and, being a suburban kid, we did't have much in common. We talked about how to play our hand with the insured.

"Miss Cresson, you really have only one choice here and that is to tell us the truth. Otherwise, the train will leave the station and you won't be on it. We wouldn't be able to help you then," James said.

I sat still, perched on the end of the bargain basement hand me down sofa in her sparsely furnished living room. James was across from her in a non-matching upholstered chair. She was next to me with the summons and complaint shaking in her hands. Her day had just gotten a lot worse and we were the cause of it. It was hot and she couldn't afford an air conditioner.

James fanned through the claim file and said, "each time the mail was used, it was a felony count with jail time and it carries a pretty hefty fine." He paused, waiting for her to do the math.

She looked at us and burst into tears. "It was big Bertha's

idea, she told me that it was easy money. We all sat around her dining room table and made it up. I met the people I was supposed to hit and everybody was laughing and pretending that their backs hurt already. We took the cars out to where it was supposed to have happened and waited for the cops."

"What about the damage to the cars, did you actually make contact?" I asked.

"Naw, my bumper was pushed in and the other car had been used a couple of times before," she said.

I made a mental note that four different people in the other car would have to make up how the impact occurred and what happened next, while they waited for the cops to arrive. Also, by getting the other claim files, we'd be able to see identical damage to the rear bumper of the struck car.

"Linda." James was moving to her first name now. "I need you to tell me exactly what happened from beginning to end." He laid out a pocket tape recorder on the table with the tape exposed.

he said that she was afraid of Big Bertha. James assured her that Big Bertha couldn't hurt her. He would make sure of it. On the other hand, she could be facing a federal indictment for Mail Fraud.

Big Bertha was the rock and James, with the weight of the Federal Government, was the hard place. North Philly is the toughest part of town, but this young woman was trying to scramble above the abject poverty and get ahead. She was not a player and all this talk of white-collar crime was a foreign language to her. She was not street smart. Big Bertha was recruiting smaller and smaller fish to swim in the insurance fraud pool. The two guys in her living room, as the day slowly turned into evening, knew what they were talking about.

She looked back and forth at us and took a deep breath,."What do I have to do?"

The tape recording doesn't take long. The promises of her safety took longer. That night, James returned me to my car and we talked about the next steps. I drove home along the Schuylkill River before the Phillies game let out.

Tuesday, I would have to explain it all to my bosses, but that had to wait. My wife fittingly went into labor over Labor Day weekend and my son was born that Labor Day Monday. I was a new dad with new responsibilities and all the excitement of the big case was replaced with all the emotions of being a first-time father.

When I returned to work, I learned that Big Bertha was a "runner" who brought these car scams to the office manager of the law firm. She was the buffer between the players and the law firm. She insulated the lawyers from the taint. My work was cut out for me to find and take receipt of the other accident claims involving all the players in the phantom wreck with Linda. Just as I created a typed out spread sheet and taped it together, it became obsolete when the claim files came in identifying even more cookie-cutter accidents. The number of "hitters" and "hit-ees" blossomed. Liz, the Assistant United States Attorney assigned to the case said that if the hitter and one person from the struck car confessed, she would accept that it was not an accident.

James and I poured over the claim files and picked the person with the most involvement in multiple cases. Therefore, they offered us the most to gain, because if they rolled on all their accidents, we only needed the hitter in each accident to roll to. Names on a spread sheet, in police reports and doctor's treatment notes, now began taking shape as living breathing and scared shitless street people. Most were more hardened than Linda, but they caved in when given the chance to ride on the train, rather than be stranded at the station. My worksheets blossomed with names and accidents. Today's hitter was inevitably tomorrow's hit-ee, I had to keep gathering files and zeroing in on the best persons to be interviewed. My work was taxing all my organizational skills as I tried to keep up with the speed of an investigation that was moving very quickly.

I also had to report my activity and still work on my other cases that I had pending. I got a break on the new stuff coming in when my fellow agents in the Delaware Valley started to shoulder a heavier load.

In short order, James and I tied up 26 accidents with 68 players. Only two handfuls of players were talking to us, but they were the dominos that tumbled the other cases. While we talked to them, an interesting pattern emerged. They went into the doctor's office for their initial visit and maybe once or twice again. That was it. I couldn't believe it. I gently shifted the treatment sheets over to James and he saw the Doctor's bill for 46 visits. Better still, when we questioned them about some of the dates, the players were in lock-up for some beef or out of the area visiting relatives. One woman had her baby on the morning of the date when she was listed as receiving a physical therapy treatment and TENS units treatment. Now we had a couple of medical providers in our sights. This was a totally unexpected bonus as those medical bills became additional counts in the mail fraud conspiracy

The process was becoming routine and it was not uncommon to talk to a couple players who gave up the rest of the players in all their accidents. Understand, we still had a long way to go, but this was a heady time. Both of us were working hard in our separate areas of expertise. I could not always keep up and joked that the claim files were lost in the mail. James saw the value of the work we were doing and always brought his A game. We'd meet early in the morning and talk about what presents the mailman brought me and how those pieces fit into the fraud puzzle we were filling out. We would go out and interview the latest targets into the evening.

From those living room confessions, my work mushroomed when we found out of even more accidents that had escaped our net.

Over the months, we made each case, one accident at a time. Word was getting out on the street and some of the players were calling James up so they could get on the train first. The break in the wall of silence that came from Linda Cresson's frantic phone call grew into a dam burst, but now the waters were subsiding.

Eventually, we went dry on finding more phony accidents with the North Philadelphia crew. Almost everyone who confessed put Big Bertha in the Bulls-Eye along with their co-conspirators.

No sooner than I thought we had a monster case with a couple of medical providers and the runner, I was then asked to find accidents with "Tony" and his girlfriend who lived in South Philly.

Thanks to the card filing system at the Mid-East Index bureau overlooking Independence Mall and the Liberty Bell, I quickly saw that they were just a couple unlucky people that kept getting hit in the rear end. They visited different doctors on Broad Street in South Philly, but were evaluated by the same Dr. "Buck and a Quarter" as the North Philadelphia crew. Yes, they were also represented by my favorite law firm.

I called the adjusters on those accidents and they gave me the names of the other players in the accidents that they were adjusting. I was now able to pull out the index cards of the other passengers in the accidents with both Tony and his girlfriend. I was able to paste together a new chart with 75 names on it. All were cookie-cutter rear-enders involving the same doctors and lawyers that Tony had used. As the years passed with these accidents, I saw a shift from South Philly out past the airport into Southwest Philly and Delaware county. The accidents with Tony and his girlfriend started a year before Big Bertha got her start. There were more accidents to look at with more players. If not for the connection to the law firm, this case, by itself, would be a career-maker. I was faced with the daunting task of gathering all the claim files and setting up the best candidates for James and me to interview.

The case just doubled in size and I was not getting any help. Worse, one of the agents that was taking some of my cases had just quit and the other agent and I had to take over his case load. I was totally invested in this project and was working day and night on this case, while trying to administrate my burgeoning case load. My son was colicky and sleep was hard to come by. Pretty soon, he would be walking. When he was born, I started the process of quitting smoking and took up running. I took him out in a heavy-duty stroller on my short runs around our new neighborhood in Skippack, Pa. I was farther from the city now and had a longer commute. Time had become my most precious resource.

Saturday's became a paperwork day. After food shopping and chores, I sat down to a day of typing reports, sending out file requests and rushing to the post office before my postmaster locked the door.

A blizzard was forecasted that fateful gloomy day in late March. Old man winter shook his fist at us one more time during that Winter of 1983. I made my way into James' office and to the side desk they had provided me. I gulped free Post Office coffee from the Postal Inspectors mug they had given me

My work space was piled high with files and the walls were festooned with the latest charts. I had to get ready for the parade of suspects that had agreed to sit down with us. We alternated between hitters and the choice "hit-ees". From over James' shoulder, I could see the snow falling over the river and Center City. It provided a serene dusting on William Penn's hat where he stood atop City Hall. Traffic was slowing to a crawl. The subways were still humming; however, and our guests popped out at the 30th Street Station and skated across Market St. When other appointments were being cancelled and private enterprise was grinding to a halt, not one person was going to be late for their appointment with the Federal Government.

By now, James was practiced at helping the players come to see that they only really had one choice.

The first guy sat down and, acting like a South Philly wise guy, said, "you guys have the wrong guy. This is all a big mistake."

James just shrugged his shoulders and said, "First things first."

He read aloud and pointed to each sentence on the Miranda form about the right to be silent, about anything that the guy said or did could be held against him in court, the right to having an attorney present and how the good and kindly taxpayers of the United States would pay for the guy to have an attorney present, if he couldn't afford one.

The wise guy wanna-be signed the form and shrugged. "Like I told you. You have the wrong guy."

James pointed to the charts that spelled out his involvement. He patted the files on his desk of his claims that made up part of the scheme. He slid some documents with the wise guy wanna -be's signature on them across the table. James then put the Miranda form, with the ink still drying on it, side by side with the claims form squarely in front of the guy. He didn't say anything about how the signatures matched. He let them just sit there. Without pausing, James explained what the date stamps and envelopes with cancelled stamps meant and how each mailing that supported the scheme was a mail fraud count. James then placed the signatures on the policy application to the other side of the claims forms. Matching signatures on several forms with the one he just provided us painted a pretty damning picture that we had the right guy. It was good theater.

James wrapped up with. "All I can do is tell the Assistant United States Attorney how you cooperated with us. I can't make any promises."

I could see that wanna-be's Adam's apple was bobbing up and down like a yo-yo. It was a winter wonderland outside, but he was now sweating profusely. Wise-talking changed to stuttering and stammering.

"Don't mean a thing." He was trying to convince himself as he leaned over the table, his eyes scanning back and forth over the signatures. He kept his hands in his black leather jacket and I could only imagine how tightly he was clenching his fists.

On cue, James scooped up all the documents from under the guy's gaze and said, "Your train is about to leave the station. Once it leaves, I can't help you anymore. There are other people waiting to get on."

James was not bluffing. Previously, we had watched a couple of knuckleheads walk away and refuse to cooperate.

Pity the fool that didn't take the deal. The whole weight of the Federal system would come crashing down on them, along with the testimony of their fellow passengers in the bogus accidents. Bail, lawyer's fees, and restitution cost would make their play a whole lot of misery.

We sat and stared at him. There was no need to rubber hose the guy (not that we would) or employ coercive interrogation techniques. The evidence was overwhelming. We had done our homework.

He blinked, looked at us, looked at the ceiling, and looked at his feet.

Glad I wasn't in his shoes.

He folded his cards with a loud exhale. "Fuckin' Tony said it would be a piece of cake. We could all make a little cash by pretending to be in these fake accidents." His hands came out of his jacket, his elbows went to his knees and his sweaty hands went his head.

James nodded to me. He was allowing our new friend to retain some shreds of his manhood. James started the cooperation letter. We slapped a fresh tape in the pocket recorder on the desk and I took over the questioning on each misrepresentation about the claims and, as importantly, the medical treatments or more appropriately, the lack there of.

By splitting the work in half, we adroitly processed the wanna-be wise guy turned "cooperator".

The morning continued with more players coming in and confessing. A quick sandwich at lunch from the cafeteria and then back at the process in the afternoon. Our appointments ran into the evening. When the last one left shortly before 8PM, we were exhausted. 11 suspects came in and 11 cooperators left. In one long day, we received confessions on 17 accidents involving 54 people and three more medical providers.

The wind was whipping the snow into drifts and there was no sign of it letting up. I would take the train out to my buried car out in the burbs.

"Ya know James, a guy could work his whole career and never have a day like this," I said.

He replied, "I know, but we still have a long way to go if we want to penetrate the law firm."

"Still, It's not a bad day's work, especially for a snow day." I counted out loud from my spreadsheets the names of 54 people in the net.

We stared out at the swirling snow and realized we may never get another case like this in our lives again.

The number of players from South and Southwest sections of the city eventually grew to 89, but there was no time for a breather when the runner in West Philadelphia was identified; then a runner in Kensington. The former group were Working-Class Blacks and the latter poor Irish and Polish. The number of suspects rose to 250 with 5 doctors and 4 runners squarely in our sights.

It was about that time that my adventure on this case almost came to an end.

"Waddayamean they denied my request for a second filing cabinet? Where am I supposed to keep all these files?" I asked my Regional Manager. It was rare for him to call me and not go through my Area Supervisor who was very supportive.

"There is no precedent for a Special Agent to have two filing cabinets," he said.

"There is no precedent for this many possible indictments in one case either," I shot back.

"The other thing John, is that I'm being told that you are ignoring your other cases, he said.

"Really? Are you kidding me? I completely worked down

my pending except for two cases that I had before this bomb exploded. I picked up Mike's cases and am working them. Every quarter, I go over to a storage unit in Jersey and type up status reports of 'No Activity' on cases of Tom and Charlie who quit and haven't been replaced. Tell me again how this is all my fault?" I was getting hot.

"When are the indictments that you keep promising going to be handed down? All those insurance companies that you've been asking files from want to know when they are going to be able to sue for restitution," he volleyed back.

"How the hell do I know? Every month, I report what I work on. The Grand Jury proceedings are secret. I don't get briefed about what is said in there. I get told 'John, you look for South Philly accidents. You look for West Philly accidents. John, can you find accidents in Kensington? I've been hustling for over a year now working this case most time and my pendings when I can, all the while babysitting those files in Jersey. And don't think I'm not hearing it from the carriers too. Every time I request a file now, I have to hear it from the adjustor. They keep a file diary and have to report to their superiors as well."

"I've given you a lot a leeway and I have to answer every month why this case hasn't produced any arrests yet," he said.

"I'm hearing about numbers. Numbers of pendings. Number of arrests. That wasn't important when we talked to Postal two years ago about focusing on this law firm. If we neutralize this law firm, it sends a real message to the rest of the law firms in this town that playing with staged accidents is playing with fire. You know the big picture stuff. Christ."

I then mumbled to myself.

"What was that you said?" he demanded.

"I said, He wants me to hand out parking tickets when I'm trying to solve a murder case."

I could tell he was pissed at me when he slowly and evenly said, "You are to begin working all your caseload and report progress on each case. Is that understood?"

I let that hang for a long moment. I had a young child. I was paying for daycare. I had a new house and a steep mortgage payment. We had two cars and car payments. "Yes sir."

That was on a Friday. Over the weekend, I talked to my wife and all the stress and exhaustion spilled out. Yeah, no shit. My ego was bruised. I couldn't imagine how I could continue to support this case without working 80 hours a week with no overtime pay. My wife worked and we were a young family. I wasn't about to turn that part of my life off. I was completely at a loss how to satisfy my boss and stay on the case.

On Monday, I followed James on the subway down to the Federal Building at 6th & Market. He was puzzled why I needed to talk to Liz.

I recounted for them the conversation I had with my Regional Manager. I was frustrated and very emotional. They understood what my continued involvement in this case meant. They clearly grasped that no one in their employ could know how to do what I did. It was a lot of grunt work that had to be done right and it always had to be done right away. They were as shocked as I was.

I was fighting back tears when I said, "If I want to keep my job, I can only give you one day a week. I think Monday's are best." And with that I fled her office not wanting them see a grown man cry.

I went back to James' office and began trying to throw all the balls in the air so I could catch them during the week and be able to move forward the following Monday. He returned later in the day and we talked some more. We both knew the importance of what we were trying to accomplish. He admitted that some petty jealousies were popping up with his fellow inspectors, but for the most part, he was allowed to work this case full-time. He learned that his boss put in for him to get some extra help. I apologized for being emotional, but I didn't know what other options I had. He said not to lose hope and that maybe Liz could do something.

Later that afternoon, I went home and needed to go for a run before dark. By then, I was up to running 10K's on the weekend and had thoughts of running a marathon. If anything, the running had kept me sane. I was putting on my shorts and singlet while listening to messages on my answering machine. It was the usual day to day stuff until about 3PM when the message came in from my Area Supervisor to call him right away. He repeated the message every half hour with more and more urgency in his voice and finally left his home phone number on the last message.

"What's up Boss?" I asked.

"What the hell did you do today?"

"I went in and told James and Liz that I had to start working my pendings and I couldn't babysit the cases left by Tom and Charlie anymore."

"You told them you could only work one day a week on their case. Right?" It was more of an accusation than a question.

"Yeah, I looked at everything and figured out that if I try to work the incoming for four agents until three could be replaced as the work came in, I will slowly work off Tom and Charley's pendings until they were gone. It was a start. I figured I could give them a legitimate one day a week while still processing what came in on nights and weekends on their case. I couldn't quit the case completely. Why? What happened?"

"You didn't need to be so theatrical. You could have just stopped showing up as much and they would have figured you were busy on other stuff," he said.

"These are people that I work with every day. I'm part of a task force. How could anything be more important than this case? How could I do that?"

"You started a shit storm. That female prosecutor you work with down there called the Director and asked him if he knew that by pulling you off their case that it was going to jeopardize the investigation. She wanted to know why other agents couldn't be called upon from New York or Maryland to handle the other cases while you worked on their case full-time. She also made it clear that the case was progressing and she would personally mail him the press releases as they were sent out. She praised your efforts and commitment to the case and said that they couldn't have made it without you always being right there with the files they needed when they needed them. She said that you have demonstrated a grasp on the investigation's objective and was pro-active, especially when it came to the medical providers."

"She did?" I asked.

"That's not all. She must have given an earful to some of the Claims Vice-Presidents that sit on our board of directors. She told them that the best insurance fraud case in the country was being messed with. They then started calling the Director wanting to know what was going on"

"Holy Shit!" I said.

"Both I and the Regional Manager were summoned to Headquarters and had to do some real fast explaining. She must have told the Director that she would be hard-pressed to take another case from us, if we pulled the rug out from under this one. How could she trust us to be there on the other cases? She also said that there is every indication that this case was going to be a blockbuster. She made it clear that she needed you full-time. She didn't know why you were still being assigned other cases. She gave the Director a real ass-chewing and it didn't take long for that grief to start rolling down hill."

"Oh."

"You really rolled the dice on this one partner. Let's hope for your sake you didn't roll snake eyes."

"Does that mean I am getting my second filing cabinet?" I asked.

"You asshole," he chuckled.

I went back to almost full-time on the case. The files would be housed at Postal. James got his helper, Chris. Liz received a second Assistant U.S. Attorney, Glen.

The work got harder as each player's case had to be tightened down completely.

As promised, Liz delivered. Later in 1983, both the North Philly and South Philly players were taken down along with their runners. In 1984, West Philly, the medical providers and the other runners were indicted.

More importantly, in the culmination of the indictments, the law firm's office manager and two of the attorneys were indicted as well.

Most surprising, was the RICO count. It was the first time that a Law Firm's assets were frozen under the Racketeering Influenced Corrupt Organization Act. Usually saved for Organized Crime, this was a powerful weapon and its broad powers opened up a whole new way of looking at the fraud rings preying on the Property & Casualty insurance industry.

The final tally was 186 players, 5 runners, 5 medical providers and 2 lawyers. I guess what was most surprising for me was that the professionals, with their licenses to print money, had succumbed to a greedy cash grab.

On the Wednesday before Thanksgiving 1984, one knucklehead decided to go to trial. We had to scramble to alert every record keeper of the cases he was involved in. One adjustor had gone duck hunting and we had to convince that insurance company's HR to call his wife and get a message to him that on Monday he had to be in Philadelphia for a Federal trial.

At the time, it was the largest fraud case in Pennsylvania history. It was so big, that they had to stop indicting the players when the Federal Probation Department cried uncle. They couldn't handle the volume, even though we worked to get the evidence on 250 players. The lawyers and law firm's office manager's cases ended badly for them and the law firm's assets were confiscated by the Government.

My company's Director was able to turn it into years of sensational PR. The Regional Manager got promoted. My Area Supervisor took his spot. For the rest of the decade, Minor Impact Soft-Tissue claims in Philly dropped to almost non-existent levels. The auto claim volume overall was much lower than similar markets. It resulted in millions of dollars in savings to the Insurance industry.

For me, it was a different story. After two years of minuscule raises and ridiculously long hours, there was a big let down. I made sure that my work was done on the case before I resigned and took another and much better-paying job with more regular hours in the industry.

- About six years later, James was a featured speaker at a Fraud Conference in Seattle that I was attending. Unfortunately, a really bad case of food poisoning put him in the hospital. I was his only visitor for a couple days and he was able to fill me in on his life since our case together and we were able to reminisce.

- A few years after that, Liz, by then in private practice working for insurance companies on fraud cases and civil RICO cases, was called to New Orleans where we were both consultants on an electrifying case together.

I KNOW KWAME

Every Criminal Defense Murder Investigation is different, yet many of the steps remain the same. You examine the police reports and look for inconsistencies. You interview the defendant. You visit the crime scenes, months after the crime scene tape is removed and take your own photos. You canvass the area for witnesses. You do background investigations on and re-interview the known witnesses. You look at the forensics and see if a forensic expert needs to be brought in to challenge the methodology or the science. You talk to alibi witnesses, No, autopsy photos are not fun to look at. Talking to friends of the victim usually falls under the law of diminishing returns. But, if you follow the steps and put forth a genuine effort, sometimes Lady Luck will smile on you, as happened in this case.

The attorney who hired me was acting as a Special Public Defender (SPD). She was appointed by the State to represent a Co-Defendant in this murder. She was being paid far less then she was worth on the State's dime and she hired me to work with her. The State rate for investigators was 79% below my normal hourly rate. I joked with her that the SPD cases were not quite Pro Bono for me, but was more like Low Bono.

Neither one of us soft-pedaled these cases. A man's freedom was at stake and the family of the dead deserved that justice be served fairly so that closure and grieving could begin. She had handled countless criminal cases by that point in her career, went to trial on some and had a good track record. She had been trying me out on some of her easier cases for a few years and was one tough cookie. I learned early to admit fault and take my lumps when I screwed up. I was learning from the best and my ego didn't get in the way. I was new to criminal defense investigations. More so, she genuinely believed that this client was telling the truth and that he had nothing to do with a brutal killing.

According to the police reports, three young men walked up a city street with the intent to rob someone. One of the boys had a gun. Supposedly, one watched from a short distance away, while the boy with the gun tussled with the driver of a parked car, then he shot him. The third boy then reached into the car and grabbed the dying man's wallet. They all ran off together at the next cross street.

I canvassed the street for two days and didn't come up with any new leads. I was rebuffed in talking to the boy who allegedly watched it happen. He had given a statement to the police that was contrary in part to that of other non-involved witnesses. Other witnesses said that he may not have even been there. His father made it clear to me that he was not giving his permission for me to talk to his son. I wanted to ask him more questions about the chronology of events before, during, and after the shooting. He had told the police that as he walked up the street, he saw a friend's girlfriend sitting on the porch and talked with her. He named her.

Compounding this boy's statement to the police, were two confessions made by the alleged shooter and the alleged accomplice, who was our client. Once arrested, both boys recanted their confessions. Looking at the three statements, I began to notice inconsistencies between them and with the non-involved witnesses. There was no CSI forensics tying either boy to the shooting. In fact, a gun was recovered a short while later in a different boy's hand when he was found dead. Ballistics put the bullets in the dead man as coming from this .44 cal Bulldog. Oh, I should add, the boy with the gun had a cousin whose palm print appeared on the passenger side of the dead man's car. These two cousins lived together with their grandmother in a house in the direction where the non-involved witnesses said the killers fled. Why wasn't more investigation into these suspects undertaken?

I tied down two alibi witnesses for our client into statements that they and our client were at a nearby pharmacy and when they heard the commotion, they went to the scene to find out what happened. That was helpful, but not enough.

A young girl was identified by the police as the girl sitting on her front step when the "boys" walked up the street. She couldn't describe them to the police and only took notice when the shot rang out 60 yards up the street. She was quickly discarded and was never approached with separate mugshot arrays that should have included our client and the alleged shooter. This baffled me. Why not tighten up the confessions with an eye-witness who saw them walk right past her?

Her mother was not responding to my cards left with other family members each time I visited their house mid-block of the street where the shooting took place.

Finally, on a Sunday, I drove over to this not so nice neighborhood in the dead of a cold winter night and tried again. This time, mom and daughter were home. I told them I just needed to clarify a question.

"How many boys walked up the street before the shooting?"

"Just two. I didn't recognize either one."

Not three.

"Did you talk to either of them?" I asked

"No."

I nodded my head. *Bingo.*

This conflicted with the third boy's statement. It took a little cajoling, but I was able to convince mom to allow me to take her daughter's statement in Mom's presence. Since the attorney I worked for agreed with my second grade parochial school teacher, Mrs Wright, that my handwriting was chicken scratch, I lugged out my laptop with a portable printer and all the wires for connection and power. I typed one sentence at a time to their verbal agreement and at the end, the tech gremlins were sleeping and a neatly word-processed statement printed out. It was signed by her and witnessed by Mom.

I was packing up and saying my goodbyes. "Thank you very much for helping me on this. It's going to mean a lot to our client." He has protested his innocence from the day one." I put on my overcoat and was about to leave.

"What I told you is the truth. I only saw two boys walk up the street that day and I didn't talk to either one of them," she said.

"Kwame will appreciate that you took the time to talk to me," I said.

"Kwame?"

"Yes, Kwame (I said his last name) is the client of the attorney I'm working for. Why do you ask?"

Then she blew me away.

"I know Kwame, I went to grade school with him. He wasn't either of the boys that walked up the street that day."

"Are you positive?" I asked.

"Positive."

I pulled out the statement and she and Mom amended it.

Not to leave you hanging, Kwame was acquitted a few months later in May of 2008 when the defense attorney shredded the State's case and I was there sitting second chair. His trial and what happened with the co-Defendant's case is a story for another day. It is well documented by Nicholas Davidoff, a Pulitzer Prize nominee in THE OTHER SIDE OF PROSPECT. I was treated fairly and accurately.

THE (H)AIR BAG INCIDENT

Talk to me. C'mon talk to me. I was staring at his brand new 1994 Chrysler Sebring in the parking lot of his condo complex. It had a perfect U-shaped crumple of the front bumper and engine compartment that was the result of collision with a telephone pole a couple of weeks earlier.

It should have been a simple collision claim, but no, its owner, who insured it with the company I worked for as a Special Investigations Unit (SIU) investigator, had a different story. I was about to meet him for a recorded interview and was staring at the car, trying to imagine what really happened.

The air bags had gone off and the fine dust from their sudden inflation coated the interior of the car's windows and upholstery. Mr. Insured told the claims adjustor that he had been drinking at a bar twelve miles away and was too drunk to drive home. Let's call him Billy. Billy called a friend to pick him up and bring him home. The next day, the local cops were banging on his door. In his hung-over state, he supposedly learned that the car had impaled itself against a telephone pole about a half mile from his home. He told the cops that he left the keys in it, as was his custom and was too drunk the night before to lock it up and pocket the keys. They were skeptical, given that the car thief drove the car from the bar to within walking distance of its owner's home. That is when they contacted us.

Okay, Mr. Hot Shot Investigator, what really happened? He drove the car home, passed out behind the wheel, and woke up when the air bag smacked him in the face. He crawled home, but had enough sense to leave the keys in the ignition so that the thief didn't have to defeat the ignition system. The air bag hit the driver of the car in the face. Too bad the driver's face didn't leave an imprint on the bag. The cops didn't say anything about him having scrapes or abrasions. So he claimed that he wasn't driving. Somebody drove him home. That was the lie. That didn't happen. That is what I had to work on.

I was let in by a woman who didn't make eye contact with me. She hurried out the door. *Strange.*

"I already told the cops what happened and I gave a phone statement to the adjustor. I want to get paid. That's what I pay insurance for, right?"

"Billy, that same policy of insurance that you purchased has a cooperation clause in it where you agree to participate in the investigation of your claim. Let me read it here on the recording."

There weren't many pleasantries when I first met him. He was younger than me, but had a beer gut and blood shot eyes. His mullet hair cut and long sideburns and mustache gave him a biker look. He was a short haul truck driver who worked nights. This interview was cutting into his sack time. One thing for certain, I understood his motive for his contrived story. If he got busted for DWI or DUI, he'd lose his Commercial Driving License (CDL) and his livelihood. He didn't want to admit to leaving the scene of an accident either. The car thief story was the phony pony he wanted to ride to town.

"So tell me about where you were that night?" I asked.

"Why? What's that have to do with anything?" he replied.

"Where do you claim the car was stolen from?" I asked.

"The Choir Stalls in Derby," he said.

"Do you think it's possible that a guy drinking there took your car?"

"It's possible, I suppose," he said.

"So if you tell me about your night there, I might be able to figure out who took your car."

So he did and I questioned him very closely about his time getting plastered at the bar. He remembered it pretty well and this formed the baseline of truthful responses I was looking for so that I could compare it with what was about to come next.

"So who did you call to come pick you up?" I asked.

Before he could reply his wall phone in the kitchen rang. I paused the tape. He went to answer the phone.

"Hello, It's Billy. Who's this?"

I could hear him talking in hushed tones in the other room.

"No, he didn't leave yet." Then there was a pause.

"He's asking me every question in the book." Pause.

"I don't how much longer." Longer pause.

"Look, I'll call you when he leaves. Yeah, love you too."

My eyes drifted over to the mantle where the wedding pictures were prominently displayed. She didn't want to be here while I was here. I didn't have to wonder why.

"Everything okay, Billy?" I asked.

"Yeah, I'm good." He sat there waiting for me to turn the recorder on.

"So, who picked you up?" I asked.

"Why do you need to know that?" he asked.

"Because, I will need to interview him or her as well," I replied.

I put him on the spot. He wasn't prepared for that question from me. He had told the cops that it was his friend Manny and I wanted to see if he would tell me that it was Manny who was the Good Samaritan.

"Manny."

"What's his last name?"

"Salvado."

And so it went on and on. One word answers prefaced by a sigh of irritation. I was bleeding him dry, but the part that I thought would give me the most fodder for further examination was the ride home from the bar.

"So you got in Manny's truck. Tell me about the ride home?"

"Whaddyamean?"

"What didn't you understand about that question?"

Of course, the ride home didn't happen and he knew that I would be questioning Manny about this part of his story. He wasn't sure that Manny would go along with this ruse and he couldn't be sure that he could get to Manny before I did and that was searing his brain right now and that is why he was trying to buy some time.

Up to this point, his memory was pretty good. Now, he came up with a perfect answer. If we were playing chess, he took my queen and put me in check with one move.

"I dunno. I was really drunk, too drunk to drive. I don't remember getting into his truck and how I got home. All I know is, the next morning the cops were banging on my door and I had a terrible hangover."

The interview didn't go on much longer after that. I had

to go to plan B, but I needed permission first from the claims supervisor.

I told Billy that I had to run out to my car and that I would be right back.

I talked to my claims supervisor and briefed him on my play and came back in.

"Do you have a Baggie?" I asked.

"What do you need a Baggie for?"

"Can you get me a Baggie, please?" I insisted.

He went to the kitchen and came back with one and a puzzled look on his face.

"I need you to pull a few hairs from your head and mustache and put them in there."

Before I could give him yet another reason to ask why I charged ahead.

"You see, we need to get a control sample from you of your hair to rule you out as the driver of the car that drove your car eleven and half miles from the bar to the telephone pole a half a mile from your home."

I held up my hand to ward off any protest or questions. I pulled a Baggie from my pocket.

"You see. I pulled these from the airbag. When the airbag hit the driver in the face, it expanded and the stitching of the airbag tightened on the face of the driver and pulled off hair from the driver's head and face."

I paused for dramatic effect.

"I am going to give the samples to the State Police lab and have them do a DNA test to see if they have the thief's DNA in their database. I need your hair sample to rule you out."

Check! I could tell that I had him by the look on his face.

"Somebody making a legitimate claim wouldn't have a problem with giving me the sample, because the airbag didn't hit them in the face. That's not the case here. You didn't want to get pinched for driving drunk and lose your license. If you lost your license, you would lose your job and your ability to earn a living." I let that sink in.

"Billy, If you told the cops that you walked home after the accident because you weren't thinking right, you could have just made a collision claim. People fall asleep behind the wheel all the time. You would have been scot free. Instead you told the cops, the insurance adjustor, and me that you weren't driving and you made a theft claim and a theft report."

I slid the claims withdrawal form across the coffee table and put my pen on top of it.

"Sign it and everything stops right here. Nothing goes any further. I don't need your hair samples, I took what I needed from the car in case you changed your mind. Billy, you can tell your wife that she can come home now. She couldn't sit here watching you lie. That is why she left. Isn't it?"

"Who will pay for my car?" he asked.

"You will, because you screwed up when you started lying to everybody. You can look out your window everyday to remind you of that. Listen, I know a couple body shops that will do it for cash and give you a break or pay it off on a credit card over time. Think of it as a penalty tax. You can always work more hours to get it back on the road."

"When they told me that the company's SIU investigator was coming out to talk to me, I got sick to my stomach. I've been sick all week thinking about it," he said.

"Imagine convincing your buddy Manny to be accessory to insurance fraud, a felony. You really didn't think that out. Did you? You will feel better by doing the right thing and then you can do the right thing by her." I said pointing at the mantle where the smiling couple looked back at me.

He read it, signed it and blew a deep breath of relief.

I walked out the door with the claim withdrawal form securely in my brief case.

I also thanked the Sebring for telling me what had really happened. I just had to listen.

ON THE SPOT

I had spent much of the previous Friday loading the ammunition that the attorney was now firing at the witness on the stand.

I was working for a Criminal Defense appellate attorney on a wrongful conviction case. The guy on the stand was the original Criminal Defense trial attorney that had pled his client into a thirty-eight year sentence for a crime that the client didn't commit. Part of the appeal dealt with how the attorney provided ineffective counsel by not hiring an investigator at all. When he pled the defendant out to jail for the rest of the healthy part of his adult life, he did so, without considering about twenty-one investigative steps.

"How much longer counselor?" the judge asked.

"Just one more question your honor." the attorney replied.

"So is it fair to say, that by failing to undertake any investigation, you acted prematurely in pleading out your client?" he asked.

The client, wearing faded orange prison garb, was sitting

next to his new attorney and waited for the answer. It was six years late, but he was now getting his day in court.

"I supposed so," the attorney on the witness stand answered.

"Is that a yes?"

"Yes."

"Cross-examination will commence after lunch," the judge banged his gravel and dismissed court.

As we gathered our papers up, the attorney stepped off the witness stand and came down to our table. His expression was neutral and hard to read, but after rotating on the spit above hot coals for a couple of hours, I was anticipating that he would have a few choice invectives for us.

Instead he asked, "Where are we going for lunch?"

Lawyers are a strange breed.

About 15 minutes later, there I was, sitting across from that attorney at the only luncheonette in downtown Rockville, CT. It was awkward to say the least. I was marketing my new PI business, after having to shut down my Missing Heir research firm. I was focusing on local attorneys with Personal Injury and Criminal Defense practices. I was a solo now, trying to grind out billable hours again. The team I was a part of could open many doors for me, but not with an attorney like this. I was determined to only open my mouth to eat and drink.

The server took my menu last and as I reached for my cup of coffee, the attorney staring across the table at me asked, "So you would have done all that work on that case?"

I nodded. To make matters worse, both of the lawyers on our team began telling him of some of the attorneys I had worked for previously and the successful outcomes we had.

Impressed, he said, "I have a murder case right now that

I could use your help on. Can you swing by my office later this week and talk with me about it."

Right situation, wrong prospect

"Sure," I said and we exchanged cards.

He was a chain smoker and his office reeked of nicotine. The film on the leather chair I sat on was transferring on to my suit. With the smoke swirling about, I knew that my garb was going right back to the dry cleaners. He sat at his desk smoking. Discovery was completed and he was facing a trial deadline in 90 days.

"He says he has an alibi for the night in question. He was with his girlfriend and her father at a car show in Meriden. I'd start with that," the attorney said.

"What's the State's case?" I asked.

"My guy came into town to settle an argument with the victim. They both pulled out their pistols and starting shooting. The vic got hit and dropped his gun. The vic staggered off to a parking lot and fell down and that's where he died." The crime scene photos were fanned out on the table for me.

I flipped through them. Nighttime with the body, daytime without. Then there were the photos of the spent cartridges in the grass by a wooden fence and a bloody gun at the beginning of the blood trail. Yellow markers enumerated each item that I would later see noted in the evidence log.

"My client's aunt was outside and said that she hid behind a tree about ten feet away from a dumpster that they were standing behind, when the argument escalated into gunfire. She waited until her nephew fled and she ran back home." The attorney handed me the transcript of the statement and the DVD of her interview.

"What time did this happen?" I asked.

He pulled out the arrest affidavit. "Midnight."

"Midnight? What is she doing out there at midnight?"

"Probably looking to score drugs," he replied.

In that crime-ridden neighborhood anything was possible. I often said that if the cops left up the crime scene tape of every shooting and murder in the last decade, the roads in this part of New Haven would be impassable. I remembered that 2010 was a pretty violent year. The gangbangers heated things up and some of the feuds had turned deadly.

He continued, "later she recanted her statement. Said that the cops pressured her into it."

"Is there any evidence to corroborate that she didn't see it?" I asked.

He shook his head, "No."

"You know what the State is going to say. The witness's statement was made at the time of the shooting and now she is waffling under family pressure."

He was impressed with my understanding of the law in this regard.

He asked, "so how do we prove that she didn't see it?"

"I'd like to come back to go through your file and make copies of what I need. Then, I want to talk with your guy. Where do they have him locked up?" It was given that the client couldn't bond out on a million dollar bail.

"Big Cheshire."

I nodded. Big Cheshire was a tier two facility, not a max or a supermax, but certainly not a country club. Little Cheshire, on the same grounds, was reserved for young teenagers charged with serious crimes.

"After digesting your file and talking to your guy, I want to walk the scene. At that point, I can give you my preliminary findings and game plan. How's that sound?" I said.

Realizing that I didn't take his suggestion about the alibi

witnesses and still smarting from the verbal whipping he got on the stand, he said, "alright. You're the expert."

Reviewing all the materials sent to defense counsel was a lot like putting together a table top puzzle where some of the pieces were missing. I had more questions when I finished. I watched and re-watched the DVD of the eye-witness's statement. She was a shabbily dressed sorrowful creature. She looked much older than her stated age. She sat slumped over, almost like she wanted to lay her head on the table. She clearly did not want to be sitting in a window-less room at police headquarters answering questions and making statements against her nephew. The transcript didn't leave anything out. I couldn't make out any of her mumblings any better than the poor transcriptionist.

I read about how the uniform cops went door to door canvassing for witnesses. That is how they learned from neighbors on a side street that the eye-witness was telling people that she saw the shooting. That is what led the detectives to her and her free trip downtown. They got what they wanted.

I read about the shot-spotter system. Electronic listening posts set up around the city could triangulate the exact location of gunfire. This was something new that was implemented while I was chasing missing heirs around the world. The shot spotter detected the gunfire at the scene, but placed it at a non-existent address.

Technology!

Big Cheshire sits on a hill, 300 yards back from the street. It's a huge dull red brick three-story building that stares silently at traffic below, sending a strong message of punishment. You don't want to be sent here, its foreboding turrets warn.

Getting permission, setting the appointment, signing in,

walking through metal detectors and entering the bowels of this penitentiary, um I meant to say correctional facility, is part of why the criminal justice system is in need of over-haul. Too poor to pay for bail, the innocent until proven guilty are housed with the proven guilty. They eat the same food, live in the same conditions, breathe the same recycled jail air. There is some cosmetic attempt to create the impression of separation, but the visiting rooms are the same for both and that is where I waited for him.

Of course, they didn't tell him that he had a professional visit, so he was unprepared. I had set up the appointment for a date before my letter would have gotten to him telling him of my appointment as the criminal defense investigator.

"My name is John Hoda." I shook his hand and we sat down.

I handed him my business card, brochure, and let him look at my State issued PI License. After all, they took away his access to the Internet, so he couldn't check me out on the web later.

What a place to hand out marketing materials, I mused, as he scanned everything.

"I've been hired to assist your attorney with your case. All my reporting goes to him and I only take direction from him. You will tell me of your innocence and I don't doubt that. The State has the burden to prove its case beyond a reasonable doubt. It's my job to uncover reasonable doubt. We will get into your alibi, but for now, I want you to tell me why your aunt would put you in the jackpot?"

I sat pen poised above my notepad with his aunt's transcribed statement next to it.

He looked at me and looked at my materials. He tried sizing me up as best as he could.

"She's the neighborhood snitch. She walks around

getting in everybody's business. She does it to keep the cops off her back when she's using."

"Do they pay her or give her drugs?" I asked.

"I don't think so, but she gets in trouble so much that she plays her information like a free get out of jail card."

He went on to tell me how many years his aunt was using drugs and drinking, getting clean and sober then relapsing.

"Why you?" I asked.

"I don't understand what you mean."

"Why did she say you did it? It sounds like she listens and watches, then stores that information up and uses it when the cops want to rain on her parade," I said.

He said, "people on the street were saying I did it. She picked up on that and when they picked her up, that's when she made up that story." He pointed at her transcript.

"Again, Why you? Why would the street start rumors that you did it?"

"We was friends. I would have never done that."

"Understand, part of my job is to develop alternate suspects. Who would put six bullets in him? I asked.

"Everybody was making him out to be a saint, but he was beefing with other crews."

"Was he a player?" I asked.

He didn't answer. That was his answer.

"Look", I said, "part of my job is to figure out how the cops got it wrong. If somebody started the rumor to throw the cops off their scent and on to you, then I've gotta figure out who and why."

He didn't answer. I guess there were people whom he feared more than the prospect of spending the rest of his life in jail.

"Okay, so tell me about your alibi?"

So he did.

I couldn't make sense of what I seeing at the crime scene. I stood behind the tree where I imagined the eye-witness said she was standing. It was the closest tree to the dumpster. I looked at the crime scene photos and identified the same tree and the location of where the dumpster sat 3 years earlier. The tree was 40 feet away from the dumpster, not 10 feet away. I imagined what pitch black midnight with no streetlights looked like. How could she see anything? I was beginning to think about what a lighting expert would say on the stand. We'd have to get the weather reports for the night and also determine the lunar cycle.

Where was the gun dropped? Where did the blood trail start? Looking at the landmarks in the photos, I walked away from the dumpster and kept walking and walking and walking to a location in the vacant lot on the adjoining street. I placed my cellphone on the ground where I estimated the victim's bloody gun was dropped at the time of the shooting. I put my clipboard on the ground where the blood trail started. I took out my pens and laid them on the ground where the spent cartridges were found. I took my photos from the same angle as the CSI photographer. I walked off the distance back to the tree. It was 90 feet away. There was no crime scene sketch or diagram in the police report. Nothing tied the shooting scene to the physical layout behind the dumpster. The distance to the dumpster on a different angle was slightly closer. I took pictures from the tree to the shooting scene and from the dumpster to the shooting scene. The Shot spotter placed the shooting right where the CSI photos said it did and not back by the dumpster. The address listed had been where a house stood and was demolished. It was now a vacant lot.

That's when it hit me, she made it up. She assumed the

shooting happened behind the dumpster, since the victim died nearby. She improvised for the interrogation cameras. After her interview, nobody went back to the scene to do what I had just done. I guess clearing a murder by arrest was good enough for some folks.

I started canvassing for witnesses. I needed to hear from other people where they thought the shots came from. I needed to know if they saw this eye-witness fleeing the scene.

I walked the entire square block encompassing the crime scene, Finally, I arrived at the address of the witness. I was prepared to talk to her. I had run her background and knew of her recorded brushes with the law. A woman parked in the driveway and asked me what I was doing taking pictures and drawing on a sketch pad as I stood on their porch facing the crime scene. I explained that I was a criminal defense investigator working for the man that was accused of the shooting that happened in the vacant lot 3 years earlier. She was more than curious and really peppered me with hostile questions, but I stood my ground. After all, I just wanted to get it right as the case was soon coming to trial.

Turns out that she was also related to my client and was sympathetic to his cause. She just wanted to check me out. That's when she called into the house and told the eye-witness to come outside.

The supposed sole eye-witness to this murder stumbled out of the first floor apartment and sat down in a heap on a broken wicker chair. It was late afternoon for the rest of us, but it looked like her happy hour began when she woke up. Years of drugs and alcohol abuse had taken their toll on her face and body. I could not see any teeth, not that she ever smiled during the entire time I talked to her. She was drunk and belligerent. She again repeated for me that the cops pressured her to name her nephew as the killer. They really wanted him for this one, they said. I asked her if anyone was with her that night. She said no. Her sister began berating her for what she had done. She told us both to go F——ourselves and staggered back into the house. Whoever said that this work was easy?

Then, on my second visit, I talked to other witnesses who filled in the rest of the picture for me. Her neighbors that share the same porch came outside when they heard the shots and watched the neighborhood get swarmed by police cars, fire trucks and EMTs. At no time did they see the eye-witness return to the property. In the eye witness's statement, she had said that she fled the shooting scene and returned home. Other people, including, the young teenage boys tooling around on their bicycles called her a snitch and gave me examples when she snitched on their friends. Adults told me how she had once walked around the street incoherent and partially-naked. Making up stories and spreading rumors was another favorite past time of the eye-witness. I jotted down names, addresses, and phone numbers along with a synopsis of each tale. These people would be useful when defense counsel had to challenge the credibility of the State's only eye-witness.

When I showed up on her doorstep again, she made it clear that she didn't want to talk to me and zig-zagged away when I tried to engage her in giving me a signed statement.

I provided defense counsel with my findings verbally and in writing. I went to his office with my diagram and photos and laid out the State's photos as well.

He wanted me to take him to the scene of the crime. I thought it was a good idea. He needed me to take him there so he could understand it all well enough to cross-examine the crime scene techs and detectives. Then he had to know which exhibits he needed when he explained his version to the jury. He had finished picking them that morning and trial was to begin on Monday.

The State did not disclose anymore eye-witnesses to his client doing the shooting.

There were no confessions, forensics or other evidence putting his client at the scene. Unfortunately, there were no good alibi witnesses either. I had spent valuable hours trying to corroborate what they wanted to say in court. In the end, they would be called, but their value was questionable.

We had talked about his theory of defense on the ride over from his offices in downtown New Haven during his lunch hour. It was a beautiful late summer day.

The whole case rested on the credibility of the eye-witness and her statement to the cops.

So there we stood. I pointed out landmarks. I paced out distances for him. I showed him sight lines. I fixed for him where a bloody gun was found and where spent bullets had fallen. As the theory of defense started to become real in his eyes, who did he see come walking up behind me?

You guessed it. The eye-witness was wearing a dirty house dress, no bra. She was padding along on the city streets in her socks with no shoes.

Defense counsel had her on the spot, literally and figuratively. No judge, prosecutor or cops to interrupt this conversation. She still made the very poor appearance that I had described to him earlier, but she was sober and willing to talk.

She offered the same recantation she had given to me a month earlier and repeated for him that she made up the story that she had given the police.

She pointed to the tree that she told the homicide detectives she was hiding behind when she supposedly saw her nephew crouching behind the dumpster, then shoot the victim at close range six times. It was the exact same tree that I had determined from her statement. It was still forty feet away from the dumpsters.

She also told us for the first time that she had told the uniform officer canvassing the neighborhood the night of the shooting that she had only heard it from her porch and didn't see it. (In his report, she was described as a female that wished to remain anonymous.)

She confirmed for defense counsel that she had told the detectives that she heard it but didn't see it when they came around the following morning. She told us that she relented after she was taken downtown and was repeatedly told by the police that they wanted her nephew for this homicide.

In the short time that I got to know defense counsel, he was anything but ineffective. Now, he was buzzing. That weekend we worked on the case, getting it airtight for trial. He smoked at his home all the while writing down his opening remarks and questions for all the State's witnesses including our girl.

Later that week, a very sober and sullen prosecution witness flipped the tables on them. She repeated her recantation in the courtroom. Having met and talked to her at the scene, defense counsel knew exactly how to cross-examine this woman who was now his witness.

Under cross examination, the lead detective did agree that the tree was over 40 feet away from the dumpster. Crime Scene technicians testified that there were no forensics behind the dumpster and all the forensics were in the vacant lot 90 feet away.

To overcome the eye-witness's statement, sandwiched

between her two denials and five recantations, using the State's crime scene exhibits, defense counsel pointed out how far the crime scene was from where she had placed herself and the shooter.

My second canvass pulled up other witnesses who looked out to the area of the shooting when they heard the report of gunfire. They did not see the witness in the area. They knew her and spoke to her poor character and lack of credibility. Defense counsel chose not to muddy the water with tarnishing the character of his now star witness. Instead, he used the police reports of other witnesses who didn't place her or anybody else near the scene after the shooting ended.

He saved his best arguments for his Closing. He patiently took the jury through the testimony of all crime scene technicians. He reminded them of the photographs entered into court as exhibits that showed the distances from the tree and dumpster to the crime scene. He reread out loud her statement that a shooting happened ten feet away from her, near a dumpster, yet all the evidence was found in a vacant lot 30 yards away. Those facts could not be explained away. Finally, he asked if a military or police marksman could hit a moving target all six times with a pistol at a distance of 30 yards in the pitch black.

After only two days of deliberations, the jury had a verdict. We made haste to the courthouse. Our innocent until proven guilty client was brought up from lock-up in handcuffs and leg shackles. They were removed before the jury was called in.

Nothing prepares you for nervous anticipation while waiting for the jury to be seated. Finally, it was time for the Jury Foreman to announce the verdict. We stood and my thoughts raced about what I could have done differently or better. What had I missed? This is the first time I worked for this attorney. Did we communicate well enough? Did we mistakenly place all our bets on destroying the eye-witness's statement? This was an all or nothing high-stakes gamble. Either way, I would walk out and get paid, but my client's fate was written on a piece of paper in the foreman's hand.

The next morning, I walked out onto my driveway in my bathrobe with my morning brew to where the delivery guy had chucked my local paper. On that spot, I read the headlines about a murder case where the defendant was found not guilty of murder. Hey, they even spelled my name right.

SHOOT-DON'T SHOOT

It was a silly process really. A carry over from when the department first started. You would pick up your relief and brief him on what happened during your shift while he took you home. This was back when the township where I grew up was a sleepy farm community outside of Philadelphia. Times had changed. The Baby Boom combined with White Flight turned much of the fertile farmlands into endless housing tracks of cookie-cutter houses and my township became a suburb. The remaining farmland was turned into sod farms to meet the growing needs of suburban Philly. Now we had two, sometimes, three guys working a shift. The Chief, Detective, and Juvenile officer worked normal weekday hours unless something big popped and they got called out. Depending on how the shifts worked and by seniority who would pick up whom, you might have both cars traveling out of the township to pick up their relief. I often joked that it was a perfect time for someone to rob a bank in the center of town. They would get a huge head start on their getaway.

Yeah, the township had its home grown criminals and its

share of juvenile delinquency. Hard drugs had not yet made its way from the inner-city. The local kids said it was easier to score pot than buy booze underage. We had our share of felony car stops and domestic disturbances. A good bar fight would be the talk of the town for months. Overall, it was still a quiet fourteen square miles of rolling hills west of the city.

The 1976 Bicentennial celebrations had come and gone the previous year and I was no longer a rookie patrolman, but still was the youngest guy on the force.

On this particular Sunday afternoon in early fall, the foliage was gorgeous. I didn't mind driving around while the citizenry went to church and then later rooted for their Eagles during the early afternoon game. Kids were shooting hoops in their driveways while the smell from people burning their brush hung in the air. My family moved here in 1960 from Latham NY, when my Dad took a promotion to work at General Electric in their space program at the King of Prussia facility. It was a typical suburban town and I was a local kid that went away to college and now came back to work with the guys I idolized growing up.

Buddy and I just finished dropping a car off at his relief's house in East Norriton and now I was taking him to his house in adjoining Plymouth Township when we got the call.

A sharp-eyed neighbor was reporting a suspicious vehicle in the driveway of their neighbor's home on Skippack Pike. They couldn't make out the license plate on the car parked in the driveway but they reported seeing two young "Negro males" disappear around back. Their older white neighbors were not home. This two lane surface road ran East from the Pennsylvania Dutch country right through Philly to the Talcony Palmyra bridge crossing the Delaware River into New Jersey.

We had been getting clobbered by day-time burglaries with some of the actors coming from North Philly, which had the reputation as being the City's poorest and most crime-ridden part of town, just two townships away.

I was driving and we moved quickly, but without lights and sirens. We didn't need to get a complaint of racing while in another municipality.

As we entered the driveway, a beat up Chevy with mis-matching tires and no hubcaps sat in front of us. I recognized the Philly car dealership name stenciled on the rear trunk as being the same dealership where then former Phillies Outfielder Johnny Callison had sold cars in the off-season.

Buddy called in the marker plate and stayed up front while I approached the car. It was empty and I put my hand on the hood. The engine was still warm. I watched the windows of the Dutch Colonial sitting on a slight rise from the roadway. The sun had disappeared behind clouds reducing the glare and I could see into the rooms where the shades or curtains had not been closed. I did not spot any movement. I looked at the windows to see if they showed signs of being jimmied. The front door was closed and I shook the handle. It was locked.

Both Buddy and I had hand held repeaters clipped to our Sam Browne Belts. These radios connected to the radio in the car that allowed us to communicate with the County-wide dispatch system, but not to each other. As I rounded the corner to the back of the house, I saw a basement window was broken with no glass on the ground.

This is the entry point. We have a Breaking and Entering. I checked the back door. It was locked. *They're in there.*

I looked out into the yard that extended about 30 yards

to a tree line and the woods that ran long and wide for about a half mile.

Just then, the radio squawked telling Buddy to go to Channel 3 where he would get the 10-28 information on the plate. He had to go back to our police car to change channels. I moved to a spot where I could see the other side of the house and the rear. Buddy could watch the front and other side from the car. After a few minutes, he then motioned me to meet him on the driveway.

"Car comes back stolen from a woman in North Philly Friday night," he said.

"Yeah, it figures with what I got. The back basement casement window is broken out and there is no glass on the outside. The opening is big enough for a person to wiggle through," I reported.

"Okay, I'll call for back up and get Norristown's K-9s down here. Go back to where you were. I'll take the other corner," he said.

He pulled the Remington twelve gauge pump shotgun from the dash mount. I unholstered my Smith & Wesson 4" Police Chief Special revolver with six Remington 158 grain semi-jacketed .38 caliber hollow point bullets. I had two speed loaders on my belt.

At the training academy and later when I had to qualify at the firing range, we would use wad cutters on the paper targets, but saved the hollow points for pumpkins and watermelons. They weren't "hot loads", but damn close to it. They were very fast moving and would penetrate deeply., Then the hollowed lead would mushroom out shattering everything in its path. They were meant to drop a crazed assailant dead in their tracks, literally. The shotgun shells in Buddy's shotgun held double ought buckshot and could stop a car engine at 50 feet.

Having never touched a gun before the FBI instructor put one in my hands at the training academy firing range, I brought no bad habits into my training. I became a pretty good shot. It was a static range where we practiced from prone, kneeling, combat stance and marksman firing positions. We fired off our service weapons, shotguns and we even shouldered an M-16 to see what an automatic weapon recoil felt like. The bigger municipalities were only beginning to roll out Shoot-Don't Shoot courses where a control tower could remotely flip out placards with painted designs along the course. The trainee would have to make an instant decision to shoot or not to shoot. In the movies, the shooter would always take the head off a Preacher waving a bible or fail to drill the woman holding a baby in one arm and pointing a gun at him with other hand, for example.

The Pennsylvania Statutes governing Use of Deadly Force got some discussion in the training academy lectures, but far less than the time spent on the motor vehicle code. There was very little in-service training for use of force courses that an officer could attend and not every PD could to afford to train all their people.

Essentially, police officers could use deadly force to protect themselves or others from immediate serious bodily harm. Officers were also allowed to shoot fleeing felons. Fleeing bank robbers were obvious felons, but what about car thieves, burglars and perpetrators of felony property offenses? Where was the line drawn?

The shock hit me in a milli-second as I rounded the corner. The two guys that the neighbor probably saw were just now picking up speed in the backyard and were headed for the safety of the dense woods.

"Freeze!" I yelled and went into my combat stance with both hands on the wooden grip of my revolver.

They both were running side-by-side and looked at each other and turned their torsos to look at me. I could plainly make out their faces at a distance of about 20 yards in the shadowed daylight. More importantly, I was concentrating on their hands. The one of the left raised his right hand. Was he carrying anything? Was he holding a gun? In that split second I had to make a decision.

I holstered my weapon and brought up the repeater to my mouth.

"46-3 46-3"

"Go ahead 46-3," County replied.

I spit out the situation and descriptions as calmly as the adrenaline flooding my system allowed.

Buddy came running up to me toting the shotgun pointed away from us, in case he tripped. "What happened?"

"I came around the corner and saw them hot-footing into the woods," I repeated their descriptions.

We were waiting for back up and now with two fleeing felons on the loose, more cars from neighboring townships would descend on the area and we would start condoning off the woods.

Buddy started directing cars where to go, as he was the senior officer on scene. County called Graterford Prison, a maximum security facility, coincidently about ten miles west on Skippack Pike to send out their escapee force complete with hound dogs. This situation was escalating fast. We could hear sirens in the distance getting closer and closer.

Our relief heard the chatter on the radio and sped to the scene. Other neighboring departments began deploying at key locations to try to keep the net closed.

One officer from a nearby township came out of his

cruiser and racked a shell into the chamber of his shotgun with much excitement.

We're goin' Coon hunting!" he yelled.

I just shook my head.

"How come you didn't drill them when you had the chance?" he demanded.

"They weren't carrying anything when they ran away. Their hands were empty." I barked back. My adrenaline hadn't bled off yet.

One of the responding cars had put his radio on broadcast mode and the speaker blared out. "46-3, 46-3" see the man at 585 West Skippack Pike about a kidnapping."

My heart sank.

"Should have put them down when you had the chance, asshole," the coon hunter said.

Buddy and I didn't have time to have a pleasant chit chat and we sped off to the new crime scene.

"My family came to take me out to dinner when these two thugs came out of my garage with a hatchet and a crowbar and threatened to kill me if we didn't do what they said," the old man said. "They dragged me back into the apartment and tied me up with the lines from my clothes drying rack and threw me in the coat closest. I was able to get out and get to the phone. They have my daughter and grandkids."

His mouth was bleeding and the knot on his forehead was turning an ugly shade of blue. He hands were still tied behind his back, but he had been able to dial the operator and yell into the phone what had happened

We were able to get a description of the Ford Country Squire station wagon out to County who then figured out the registration plate and made the Broadcast. The kidnappers had at least a 15 minute head start.

On a quiet Sunday fall afternoon, this Be On the Look Out (BOLO) was broadcast with screeching alert tones county wide and Philadelphia PD was alerted.

The problem was compounded by the fact that many of the neighboring townships had sent what they could and those cars were now out of position to do an intercept in their own towns.

The man's daughter and her two kids were now in a car with two extremely dangerous men headed God knows where.

Being the new guy, I worked mostly midnights, weekends and holidays. I got to know some of the other guys on my township's borders who worked the same shifts as me. We'd meet for coffee and sit and talk to keep awake. One of us might be working solo on the graveyard shift if our partner booked off sick. We'd let each other know when any of us had to work solo. We'd keep an ear tuned to the radio calls of the guy working alone and start drifting over to his turf, until he cleared the call.

Just about when all looked hopeless, Frank, the part-timer from Ambler Borough, alerted County. I knew him well. He was as good as any full-time guy and cool under pressure. He kept his head in the game when the BOLO went out. He went immediately to the spot where the station wagon would high tail it back to Philly through Ambler. He told County that one was driving while the other one was sitting behind Mom next to the kids in the back seat. He initiated a soft follow with no lights and sirens. We listened as we secured our crime scenes. Frank handed off the tail to the Springfield Township and they followed without being made as the caravan entered Cheltenham Township which bordered North Philly. The takedown was going to take place before they got back into the City of Brotherly Love.

Cheltenham PD had their own radio dispatch and we went into the dark.

I wasn't quite 23 years old, with a little more than a year's experience on the job, but I didn't question my decision not to shoot when I had them in my sights. How could I have known that they would come out of the woods, hide in a garage, just in time for a family to bring them their escape vehicle? Now was not the time to be comforted by the odds, we needed a miracle.

A "disabled" city bus opened its doors from the left hand turn lane at the same time as the pick-up truck in front of the station wagon in the center lane abruptly stopped. Two uniformed policemen jumped out of the van on the right side of the station wagon. The bus emptied out five uniforms and the station wagon was surrounded and boxed in.

There was no struggle; the hostages were extricated unharmed and like that, the ordeal was over.

Our detective went there and brought the family back to our crime scene to re-unite with Gramps. Buddy and I typed out our statements, while our relief processed the burglary crime scene.

Long after my new bride went to bed that night, Jack Daniels and I replayed the scenes with couldas and shouldas until I passed out.

The fingerprints in the car in the driveway, matched up with those inside of the burgled house and those at the kidnap scene to the two gentlemen that were pulled out of the station wagon. I was able to identify them as the fleeing felons, although nothing was found to be stolen. They had staged goodies by the back door, only to spot me walking in the backyard.

They both pled guilty. Montgomery County judges did

not like people coming out to the County to commit crimes. This judge meted out harsh sentences.

*As a post script, *the Pennsylvania Legislature in the 1978 session reformed the use of deadly force statutes and removed the fleeing felon provision. What a difference one year made in split second decisions to shoot or not to shoot.*

THE FRIENDLY SKIES

"So what do you do," she asked.

We were seated side by side for the wedding reception on Mt. Desert Island, Maine near Bar Harbor. The Bridal Party was out with the photographer making memories. It was a glorious October day in 2017, when my friend and his new bride decided to tie the knot. On the way up from Connecticut that day, the fall foliage was spectacular. I reminisced with my wife about a trip to Houlton, Maine some twenty plus years earlier when the leaves blazed in oranges and reds against the evergreens. Then, I was investigating a murder. Today, I was celebrating a wedding; much better reason to be in the Pine Tree state.

"I'm a license professional investigator," I replied.

I found that explanation minimized the whole Sam Spade mystique.

"That must be very interesting," she said.

I nodded. "It's the coolest job at the Grove."

The Grove was a co-working space in New Haven where I hung my hat occasionally. That is where I knew her husband and the groom from.

So the invariable question came up. "Do you follow people around?"

I get that asked more times than I can count. I don't play to stereotype, but the movies, books and TV tend to glorify the job.

"Used to, but my son does that now and then when the need arises. He's better at it and his bladder can handle sitting in a car for long periods of time better than me."

She smiled.

I added, "we mostly work for attorneys that represent the families of people who died in horrible accidents or attorneys who represent the wrongfully accused or convicted."

It didn't take her long to process that as she told me that she was an attorney at a white shoes law firm in New Haven. I mentioned the name of a litigator there and the connection was cemented. The reception was wonderful with more food than I could eat, open bar for those who choose to partake and a kick-ass DJ. The bride and groom made a lovely couple and they kissed and danced the night away. Till death do us part. Happily ever after. After all, that is what the dream is all about, right?

For many years, I didn't wear the Rose-colored glasses when I lifted the camera to my eye to record the kissing, cuddling and the more frisky and risky behaviors in public when the errant spouses thought no one was looking. How about that time when the ex-wife left the toddlers alone in the house in the dead of night to go score Crack? I shouldn't forget to mention the time when I filmed the wife and her female friend having a play date while their kids had a much tamer play date. All my clients had suspicions and then the bad news would come crashing down on them, while they replayed the videos over and over again. Yep, the honeymoon was certainly over.

It certainly was that way for Jack during those winter days after 9/11. He was a hot shot Wall Street money guy and he knew his wife, the mother of his children, was stepping out on him while he was slaving away down in the City. They lived in a mansion in Greenwich and had everything, but happiness, I guess.

"I need the proof, because this divorce will go to trial. I have an ironclad pre-nuptial agreement that I will enforce. She will get nothing."

He was very direct and clear. They weren't legally separated and still shared the same bed. It was tough for him to go through the motions of daily living and the rare roll in the hay. He wanted to end the charade for both of them once and for all.

I was recommended to him by his lawyer for whom I had hit a home run before.

"She's flying to Chicago and is supposed to connect to a flight to her parent's house in Phoenix. I think she is just staying in Chicago.

"I want you to get on the plane with her and follow her wherever she goes," he said.

"When she gets off at O'Hare, I will need at least two maybe three guys to pick her up there," I said.

"Why that many guys?" he asked.

"I will need a guy in the terminal to hand her off to. I will be the bird dog pointing out the prey. He then foot follows her to baggage and then ground transportation. She might take the CTA into the city. That's why we start with a foot follow. What about a car service? What if boyfriend is waiting for her at the baggage carousel? It is the largest airport in the country and the roads around it are always under construction. The more assets in place during that critical phase, the better."

"You're the expert," he said.

"If she connects with another flight from Chicago, other than Phoenix, I will stay with her as best as I can, until I can get boots on the ground at her final destination."

The picture of the wife didn't do her justice. Her long blonde hair was perfectly coiffed. The mid-calf faux tan leather coat and furry hood completed the picture. I watched her approach the ticket counter at near-by Westchester County Airport from behind my Wall Street Journal. I know it is so cliché. She lifted her large bag onto the scale with ease. That time with the personal trainer who came to the house was paying off. I ambled over to the carousel and saw that the final destination for that bag was Phoenix. That threw me off. I sat back down and pondered this wrinkle. Was she really going to Phoenix or was this part of the ruse? She took off her coat and was wearing thick woolen sweater and Hermes's scarf. The jeans were high-end designer and didn't leave much to the imagination. My pedestrian knowledge of women's shoes left me wondering if the pair on her feet cost more than everything I was wearing.

We boarded and I was two seats behind her on the aisle while she had the window.

How hard was this follow?, I thought. She couldn't go anywhere now. No left turns across four lanes of cut-throat traffic. No school buses flashing red lights while your subject disappeared into the distance. No abrupt stops forcing you to drive by. Not one of the other hundred reasons a surveillance follow turns to crap. She and I were breathing the same air and drinking the same airline coffee from styrofoam cups.

I wondered if she figured that she was being followed on

the plane. I had time to call the client from my flip phone, before boarding and tell him about the luggage going on through to Phoenix. She was willing to burn the tickets to and from Phoenix, why not burn the luggage and clothes? Maybe the luggage would end up with her parents for her next visit out to sunny Arizona.

We were sticking to the plan. I had the numbers of the two PIs on the ground in the Windy City set on speed dial. I knew the owner of that firm, Bill, for many years and these ex-Chicago cops could get around the city as effortlessly as when they were on the job. Once they took over, I was done. Then the real work would begin with twenty-four hour a day surveillance until she got back on the plane to go home to the not so loving arms of her husband who would be waiting with a process server to hand her the divorce papers, if he was right about her infidelity.

I waited until she got into the aisle before I stood up. I wanted a few people (spacers) between us. When she entered the terminal, she turned away from baggage and ground transportation and picked up her pace as she walked with other travelers further down the concourse. Was the Phoenix connection at another gate? It was. I didn't know what to think. Did she make me? When I saw her take a seat at that gate, I cooled my heels in the Windy City Carvers Deli. Eventually the boarding calls were made and the line formed for first class passengers and she got into that line. *My work is done here Kemosabe,* as the Lone Ranger would say. I was not going to break off until they were wheels up.

At almost the last moment, she slipped out of line and walked though the gate areas and back on to the concourse. I got on the horn with the foot follow guy. He was out of position because he had to move his car or get it towed by the irate Transit cop who didn't give a damn about his badge. He was now circling the airport to get back into the departures lanes while the other PI was parked at arrivals.

I had to take her until she left the airport. If she took public transportation, so did I.

She took the escalator down to baggage where she walked up to a limo driver holding a sign with somebody's else name on it.

Smart.

He took her carry-on and she adjusted her Gucci bag and put on her sunglasses.

"She's with a limo driver and they are walking out to short-term parking."

"The Limo's have their own spot to sit with the taxis. Why are they going to Short term parking?" the PI asked me.

"How the hell do I know, It's your town," I said.

I stepped out of the building into the cold wind and bright sunshine. The limo driver and the wife walked briskly into the short term lot where I spotted a black Lincoln Town Car. I needed to position myself to get the license plate or else it would be just another Limo leaving the airport for the Chicago PIs.

"What's your 20? (short for 10-20 in cop speak for what's your location?)" I asked.

"I'm still hung up. I won't get there in time," he said.

"I'll get you the plate. Can you get to an intercept position?" I asked.

I was taking a parallel zig zag path through the lot. My overcoat was stuffed into my carry-on and now I was only in my business suit. I had to change my look somehow. I was the guy in the waiting room in Westchester, the guy on the concourse in Chicago and now the guy in the short term parking lot. How long would my luck hold out?

They approached the limo and he opened the back door for her, she got in and he closed it. The tints on the limo blacked out everything. I had to get to the rear of the limo to get the plates for my guys or else we would lose them.

A pick up truck was blocking my view. *Damn it!*

I started moving toward a position by the exit where the limo would have to drive by me As I moved to the other side of the side of the limo, I saw that side rear passenger door open and the wife flew out and immediately dove into the back seat of a ratty Toyota. The female driver quickly threw a blanket over the wife, closed the door and got back into the driver's seat. No sooner than she did that, the Toyota came to life and moved quickly to the exit.

"You're never gonna believe this. She just got out of the limo and dove into the back seat of a shitbox Toyota and she is covered up by a blanket."

"You're shitting me."

"I shit you not."

"It's a beat up brown Corolla with registration plate 375-3681!", I repeated it again as the Toyota idled with other cars in line to pay at the booth.

"I see you. You are wearing a gray suit. I see the car too. I got it from here," he said.

Relieved. I waited until the Toyota cleared the lot and it was not until then that the limo slowly rolled towards the exit.

"Mr Hoda. you just arrived here." the security guard supervisor said after he searched my carry-on and patted me down.

"Yes, I know, my business appointment was cancelled while I was in the air and they couldn't get a hold of me, until I landed," I lied.

"What kind of business? he asked.

"Private Investigations, my client owns a PI Firm down-town. Do you want his number?"

He seemed uncertain what to do next.

"I've got no reason to stay here, so I want to surprise my wife and kids for dinner." I showed him a Little Chicago Cubs stuffed animal for my daughter, a Cubs T-Shirt for my son and a local cookbook for my wife.

He nodded and let me through security.

I had my Chicago coffee mug in my briefcase and now it sits in my racks with the hundred or so other mugs which I've collected over the years.

Oh, by the way, the wife spent the long weekend in and out of the boyfriend's Lakeshore condominium with the boyfriend while her parents lied about her being in Phoenix.

The divorce was nasty.

THE END

Milford Elementary
One deceased groom-to-be. One dead-end clue. One last chance at redemption. Gwendolyn Strong feels lost outside the classroom. And at loose ends after retiring, the ex-kindergarten teacher longs for the excitement her stable marriage and yoga sessions can't provide. So the spirited fifty-something leaps into action when a former student takes his life on the eve of his wedding day.
Skeptical that he died by his own hand, Gwendolyn teams up with her elderly mentor and true-crime addict daughter to scour the small town for clues while dodging the dismissive cops. But when her prime suspect turns up fatally crushed in a freak accident, she fears a cunning culprit could be pulling some murderous strings.
Can Gwendolyn solve the case before her name is next on the hit list? *Milford Elementary* is the nail-biting first book in the Gwendolyn Strong Small Town Cozy Mystery Series. If you like whip-smart heroines, buried secrets, and gripping suspense, then you'll love J A Hoda's masterful whodunit.
https://geni.us/MMNE

Milford Coal & Ice

Two dead bodies are found behind a fake wall in the basement of a pre-civil war era mansion. The grisly discover rocks the world of centenarian Emelina Bidwell who believes her nephew and his wife left small town Milford fifty years ago. Former kindergarten teacher Gwendolyn Strong agrees to help her mentor, but the sleuthing rules are changed by Emelina who made promises of secrecy to the dead all those decades ago. Can Gwen solve the mysteries of their deaths with one arm tied behind her back? Who is protecting the killer a half-century later? Why does the town's power elite want to shut her down? Is she next to disappear? Can this amateur detective repeat her success In this second book of the small town mystery series

Buy *Milford Coal & Ice* (Book two) and follow the clues as Gwen heats up this cold case.

https://geni.us/dT7g

Milford Daffy Day

Sift out the clues with Gwen. A nut allergy almost turns deadly at Milford's daffodil festival. When former kindergarten teacher Gwendolyn Strong starts delving into the elderly woman's claim that someone is trying to kill her, little does she realize that the killer won't stop until they get what they are after. Is it revenge? Is it money? Things get deadly serious when they make an attempt on Gwen's life. Does Gwen have the courage to continue sleuthing? Will she be able to be able to figure out who it is before they strike again?

Buy *Milford Daffy Day* (Book three) and follow along with Gwen as she finds more ingredients of this killer's deadly recipe.

https://geni.us/zHoJ

Milford Bed & Breakfast
**No way in. No way out. Who killed the party host? Follow
the clues with Gwen in this present-day homage to locked
room mysteries of the Golden Era in Milford Bed &
Breakfast, book four in the Gwendolyn Strong Small
Town Cozy Mystery Series**
Gwendolyn Strong is invited to a sumptuous dinner. The
occasion is the grand opening of a restored Victorian
mansion overlooking the town as a bed and breakfast.
Gwen's husband Ken performed the restoration. A wealthy
stockbroker and his socialite wife invites their family, close
friends, business associates and a glamorous movie star. In
the morning, the host is found dead, shot in the head. This
locked room whodunnit pays homage to Agatha Christie
and John Dickson Carr. Can Gwen solve his murder? Phone
lines are down and the only bridge to the mansion is
washed away. The house is cut-off from outside assistance.
Can Gwen solve the murder with just what she learned?
Warning: There is a twist
https://geni.us/fDAy6As

**Odessa on the Delaware: Book One in the Marsha O'Shea
Series**
Can FBI Agent Marsha O'Shea stop a Russian gang
enforcer on a murderous spree to take over the Philly mob
scene? She made a mistake that cost the life of a crime beat
reporter, and an innocent man is being framed for the
grisly killing. Uncovering the truth may get her killed in the
final showdown. If you like crime thrillers with a mystery
twist, you'll love real-life PI John A. Hoda's debut crime
novel.

Buy *Odessa on the Delaware* and start tracking the clues with
Marsha now! https://geni.us/oHrU

Clearwater Blues: Book Two in the Marsha O'Shea Series

Can disgraced FBI Agent Marsha O'Shea, on administrative
leave, prevent her neighbor's deranged ex-husband from
shooting up a battered women's shelter? A perfect storm of
domestic violence, untreated mental illness, and lax gun
laws come together in the final deadly encounter. Can
Marsha prevent the next mass-shooting headline?
If you like determined heroines, high-stakes domestic
drama, and finding out what makes a mass-shooter tick,
you'll love John A. Hoda's domestic thriller.
Double lock the gun cabinet and buy *Clearwater Blues* today!
https://geni.us/gFRM

Detroit Wheels: Book Three in the Marsha O'Shea Series
The clock is ticking as FBI Agent Marsha O'Shea tries to
stop a mass murderer before he kills again on the same
exact date every year: 9/11. His target: Muslim women.
Marsha and her trusted sidekick Ramit grind outside of
normal channels to put together the clues as they are
ordered to avoid the local field office and other three-letter
agencies who have been spying on the citizens of Motown.
Will they stop the murderer in time? John A. Hoda pulls out
all the stops in this ticking clock thriller. Take a spin with
Detroit Wheels today!
https://geni.us/G9EP8

**West Reading Traffick: Book four in the Marsha O'Shea
Series**
Sixteen-year-old Irina Muldakova came to America to be a
model, or so she thought. Can injured and burned-out FBI
Agent Marsha O'Shea and a young, honest police officer

find Irina before she disappears again into an international sex trafficking ring run by the uber-wealthy?
Buy *West Reading Traffick* and take on the tyrants today!
https://geni.us/WH1G4yb

Elm City Towers: Book five in the Marsha O'Shea Series

Twenty years ago, Sandra Jenkins, a law student in New Haven, CT, was brutally murdered. Her alleged killers were quickly apprehended. Case closed. End of Story. That was until new evidence exonerates them and a new investigation is begun, but not by the cops. An investigative journalist turned podcaster is looking to make headlines. He is burning up social media. FBI agent Marsha O'Shea is working the case quietly as a special project for the FBI Deputy Director. As they get closer to the truth, bodies start to drop. Will Marsha find the killer before she becomes the next target?
https://geni.us/7bnIm2

Liberty City Nights: FBI Agent Marsha O'Shea Prequel Novella

Miami's most wanted drug dealer is on the run, always one step ahead of the cops. Young, newly married FBI agent Marsha O'Shea, working with the fugitive task force, has figured out how to draw him out of hiding. Will she get killed in the final showdown?

This prequel novella takes us back to the year 2000 where she earns her reputation as a gunslinger starts, but not without consequences.

Mr O'Shea wants his wife to settle down and start a family. FBI agent Marsha O'Shea is working on the Violent Crimes Squad

Bank in Miami and is making a name for herself as gunslinger when the FBI was the federal alpha dog in the fight against crime pre 9/11. There is no compromising as the sparks fly. Meet Marsha O'Shea and find out why she is driven to achieve.
https://geni.us/nlfbn

Second Chance at Bat

When a Little League coach wins a trip to Phantasy Baseball Camp, it sets in motion an unforgettable season with his beloved Philadelphia Phillies. Joe DiNatale, a thirty-nine-year-old insurance agent from Reading, Pennsylvania, discovers that he has a magical pitch, and through luck and circumstance, he receives an improbable tryout. Nobody is prepared to handle the instant rock-star celebrity, and this average joe has to hold on to his hometown values for dear life. The ride gets bumpy during the All-Star break on and off the field, setting the stage for an unforgettable finish.
https://geni.us/OXqR

No career mentor had a greater impact on me than New Haven, CT Civil Rights and Criminal Defense Attorney Diane "Cookie" Polan 3/12/51-1/21/2016

ABOUT THE AUTHOR

John A. Hoda is a real-life PI whose cases have headlined in the Philadelphia Inquirer and New Haven Register. He coaches at www. ThePICOACH.com and has written several How To books on the business of private investigations. He is an award winning writer. In 2019, he was a debut novelist, panelist and Shamus Judge at the Mystery Writers Conference in Dallas, TX His podcasts **My Favorite Detective Stories** can be found at your favorite pod catcher or at www.johnhoda.com where he can be reached.

ACKNOWLEDGMENTS

Many thanks to beta readers extraordinaire: Don Berman, Neil Olsen, Robin Vierow, Skip and Marg Zeiders and special thanks to Marg for the line edits.

Book Cover Design by www.ebooklaunch.com